Routing in Wireless Mesh Networks

Raghav Kumar

First Printing, 2023

ABSTRACT

Wireless mesh networks (WMNs) are a special case of wireless multi-hop networks. Increased number of packet transmission in Multihop communication reduces the network throughput capacity in wireless mesh networks. In the past decade, numerous methods such as multi-channel transmission through multiple Network Interface Cards(NICs), multi-path transmission and network-coding were employed to improve the throughput of WMN's.

Network coding is a method of encoding and decoding the transmitted data for the intention of increasing the throughput, reducing the delay there by obtaining robust mesh network and it has been widely used in many networks. In this work, the low network throughput problem faced in WMNs has been tackled using network-coding.

In the coding-aware routing protocol design, there are three essential aspects: 1) coding condition, which is used to effectively discover the coding opportunities, and 2) routing metric, which should carefully be designed to facilitate the routing protocol in a simple effective manner 3) The choice of determining the forwarding list and forwarding encoder node. To circumvent all these issues mentioned above, this proposed work helps to address the above issues using any path route metric, code-aware, load-aware route metric and estimation of bandwidth with a network coding to compute the gain of opportunistic transmission. To resolve the decision of which nodes should be included in the forwarding list for sending the encoded packet among all the intersecting nodes to obtain the highest throughput gain, most of the researchers considered the first intersecting node as an encoding node among all the intermediate nodes in wireless mesh networks, in spite of the quality of the first node. The major intention of this work is to consider delay and anypath cost metric in the routing path when deciding the encoding node in the opportunistic routing.

A new Opportunity Encoder based Delay Aware Routing (OEDAR) algorithm is designed using anypath routing cost in which each node performs the coding opportunity and chooses the appropriate route by itself using the information obtained from its neighbors and the feedback from intersecting nodes in its routes. To realize OEDAR, every encoded node within two hop regions will get selected and each node perform the computation of temporary anypath cost and total delay independently for each encoded flow using Optimal encoder selection (OES) algorithm. All flows constantly choose the lowest anypath cost path and minimal delay as their transmission route. Prior to network coding, the coding node must ensure whether the encoded flow is decodable which means at least one node in the backward list can be able to decode this encoded flow. To ensure this, the coding node must have the decoding knowledge before taking any coding decision. OEDAR can be able to handle diverse environments, such as multiple flow rates and multiple coding nodes along the route. Simulations of the proposed routing protocol have been carried out under NS-2 simulator. The results show that OEDAR outperforms HCOR by selecting one node that has minimum delay and lowest any path cost has been chosen among all intersecting nodes. And it shows higher throughput, low end-to-end delay and high packet delivery ratio for the proposed OEDAR algorithm.

A new improved Adaptive Coding Aware Routing (ACAR) algorithm is designed by considering anypath routing cost, delay and bandwidth of selected flow. This study also establishes and observes an optimal encoder node for two distinct flows that will not have the intermediate node in wireless mesh networks. The proposed encoder node selection algorithm is projected to improve the performance of routing protocol for the transmission of packets in wireless mesh networks. Flow Adaptive Coding Aware Routing (F-ACAR) algorithm is applied when two flows don't have the intermediate node but have the common overhearing node for anyone of the two flows. Selective flow Adaptive Coding Aware Routing (S-ACAR) algorithm is applicable only when two flows have common overhearing node in the network then it selects any one of the optimal node which should be placed in neighbour list of two flows and satisfies the coding condition. The performance results of this ACAR gives better results by improving the average throughput and packet delivery ratio and reducing delay consumption with increasing nodes when compared with existing protocol.

Network-coding combines all the packets based on the coding strategies to save the bandwidth. It should be noted that, the packets are combined only if the coding strategies are satisfied. To be safe from the packet loss, the incorrect packet encodings should be avoided and to support large number of packet encodings. It is essential to guarantee that the coding strategies employed are necessary and correct. To override these difficulties, an improved set of coding strategies has been developed to identify large number of coding structures and to support more packet encodings. It is essential to design a novel routing protocol to discover the path with more benefits riding on current network traffic patterns by utilizing the proposed coding conditions.

A proposed Network Coding Aware Routing (Net-CART) protocol in wireless mesh networks considers the scenario that more than two flows intersect at one node. An improved set of coding strategies called Enhanced Universal Coding Strategies (EUCS) is also proposed to determine large number of coding opportunities. A node in the Net-CART approach adapts the EUCS to find whether the packets can be encoded collectively or not. Beyond this newly developed coding strategy, a new metric Code-Aware and Load-Aware Route Metric (CALARM) is developed to utilize the whole goodness of network coding and enhance the network throughput. CALARM is modelled based on a small amount of transmission and consider the coding opportunities to transmit a packet from source to its respective destination. The path with minimum CALARM value is required for minimum number of transmissions to send a packet from the source to their respective destination. So that source node selects the optimal path for packet transmission. A new control packet Reverse-Route-Update (RvRoup)is employed to compute the CALARM value of a path easily and updated periodically. Using this RvRoup method, a source node receives the latest information about the network and based on the CALARM routing metric, the source node selects the most ideal path for transmission of packets. Following the basics of Dynamic Source Routing (DSR) and Free-ride Oriented Routing Metric (FORM) algorithm, the Net-CART has been proposed for perfect transmission of packets to the destination. Our proposed Net-CART algorithm attained higher throughput when compared to other existing routing algorithms. Net-CART algorithm not only identifies more coding-structures (i.e., the unique ways the packets encoded collectively) but also follows the coding-structures to generate more packet-encodings.

TABLE OF CONTENTS

CHAPTER NO.	TITLE	PAGE NO.

CHAPTER NO.	TITLE	PAGE NO.

CHAPTERNO.	TITLE	PAGENO.

CHAPTERNO.	**TITLE**	**PAGENO.**

CHAPTERNO. **TITLE** **PAGENO.**

LIST OF TABLES

LIST OF FIGURES

FIGURE NO.	TITLE	PAGE NO.

FIGURE NO.	TITLE	PAGE NO.

LIST OF ABBREVIATIONS AND SYMBOLS

AP	Access Point
ANCHOR	Active Network Coding High throughput Optimizing Routing
ACAR	Adaptive Coding Aware Routing
AODV	Ad Hoc On Demand Distance Vector
AOMDV	Ad hoc On Demand Multipath Distance Vector
BRONC	Backbone Routing with Network Coding
BS	Base Station
BLC	Bottleneck Link Capacity
BLJCAR	Buffer management Low Jitter Coding Aware Routing
CAR	Capacity Aware Routing
CSMA	Carrier Sense Multiple Access
CALARM	Code Aware and Load Aware Route Metric
COAR	Coding Aware opportunistic Routing
CIAR	Coding Interference Aware Routing
CLONE	Coding with Loss awareness
CA MPATH CODE	Coding Aware Multipath Routing
CAMP	Coding Aware Multi Path routing
CORMEN	Coding aware Opportunistic Routing in Mesh Network
CRM	Coding aware Routing Metric
CA SPATH CODE	Coding Aware Single Path routing

CORE	Combined Opportunistic Routing and network coding
CAR	Congestion Avoidance Rate
CDS	Connected Dominating Set
CFCR	Connected dominating set based Flow oriented Coding aware Routing
DSDV	Destination Sequenced Distance Vector
DCAR	Distributed Coding Aware Routing
DGCDR	Distributed Greedy Coding aware Deterministic Routing
DSR	Dynamic Source Routing
ENT	Effective Number of Transmissions
ER	Efficient Retransmission
EUCC	Enhanced Universal Coding Conditions
EUCS	Enhanced Universal Coding strategies
EAX	Expected Anypath Transmission
EATT	Expected Anypath Transmission Time
EFW	Expected ForWarding counter
ECX	Expected number of Coded Transmissions
ERC	Expected Resource Consumption
ETX	Expected Transmission count
ETCNC	Expected Transmission Count based on Network Coding
ETT	Expected Transmission Time
EXOR	Extreme Opportunistic Routing
FN	Forwarding Nodes
HCOR	High throughput Coding aware Opportunistic Routing
HWMP	Hybrid Wireless Mesh Protocol
IGCC	Improved Generalized Coding Conditions

IEEE	Institute of Electrical and Electronics Engineers
IPRA	Intelligent Portal Routing Algorithm
IAWARE	Interference AWARE
IP	Internet Protocol
IERP	Inter zone Routing Protocol
IARP	Intra zone Routing Protocol
LCMR	Light Client Management Routing
LPF	Linear Programming based Formulations
LQSR	Link Quality State Routing
LAETT	Load Aware Expected Transmission Time
LMTR	Load balanced Multicast Tree Routing
LAN	Local Area Network
MMR	Markovian Metric Routing
MAC	Medium Access Control
MRS	Mesh Routing Strategy
MIC	Metric of Interference and Channel switching
MANET	Mobile Ad hoc Networks
METX	Modified Expected number of Transmissions
MCMR	Multi Channel Multi Radio
MPATH	Multi Path Interference aware Routing
MRT	Multi path Routing Throughput
MPR	Multi Point Relay
MRA	Multi Rate Algorithm
NOCOCO	Near Optimal Coordinated Coding
NCAR	Network Coding Aware Routing
Net CART	Network Coding Aware Routing
NCRT	Network Coding Routing
NCMR	Network Coding based Multipath Routing
NIC	Network Interface Card

NJCAR	Network Joint Coding Aware Routing
NSR	Node Stability based Routing
OEDAR	Opportunity Encoder Based Delay Aware Routing
OES	Optimal Encoder Selection
OLSR	Optimized Link State Routing
PER	Packet Error Rate
PTC	Potential Transmission Count
RRNOC	Regular Routing with No Coding
RROOC	Regular Routing with Opportunistic Coding
RTN	Required Transmission Number
ROMER	Resilient Opportunistic Mesh Routing
RERR	Route Error packets
RREP	Route Reply
RREQ	Route Request
ROCX	Routing with Opportunistically Coded Exchange
SMAF	Shortest Multi rate Anypath First routing
SPATH	Shortest Path routing
SPATH CODE	Shortest path routing with network Coding
SOAR	Simple Opportunistic Adaptive Routing
TRP	Traditional Routing Protocol
TDiCOR	Transmit Diversity Cooperative Opportunistic Routing
WCETT	Weighted Cumulative Expected Transmission Time
WEP	Wired Equivalent Privacy
WBA	Wireless Broadcast Advantage
WLAN	Wireless Local Area Network
WMN	Wireless Mesh Networks
WMR	Wireless Mesh Routing

WSN	Wireless Sensor Networks
WiMAX	Worldwide Interoperability for Microwave Access
ZRP	Zonal Routing Protocol

CHAPTER 1

INTRODUCTION

This chapter emphasizes the overall introduction and basics of the network, classification of routing protocols in wireless network, network coding and its algorithms.

NETWORKS

A network is a collection of interconnected systems and it shares or communicates the information across a common transmission medium. Network can also be defined as two or more computers connected together to share the resources such as data, printer, modem, or service such as database or an email system which also interacts using a shared communications link. The individual systems must be associated through a pathway called the transmission medium which has been used to transmit the resources or service between the computers.

Companies or organization can send the same information or data to enormous numbers of employees or customers quickly and efficiently by using the network. Some examples include company newsletters and announcements for employees, as well as advertisements and purchase information for customers. Besides, an employee can communicate with other employees within the company and outside using an electronic means of communication namely e-mail that is similar to mail but done on computers, usually over the Internet. E-mail is the most commonly used feature of the Internet, and its use has been growing significantly. All the systems on the pathway must follow a set of general communication rules for data transmission from source to arrive at its destination with in time. Protocols are set of rules governing computerfor the transmission of data from the source node to the end node.

Wired Networks

A collection of two or more systems and other devices, which are linked by physical cables and network adapters for transferring the data between different devices and PCs, are known as wired networks. For communicating more computers wired LANs usually require central devices like hubs, switches, or routers. Ethernet is the fastest wired network protocol, with the connection rate from 0 megabits per second (Mbps) to 00 Mbps or higher.

All the computers are connected in a small wired network using the router or switches. In order to connect a system to a network with physical cable, the system must have an Ethernet adapter which is also called as Network Interface Card (NIC). One among these devices which typically connects to a cable modem, or other type of Internet connection, provides Internet access to all the devices connected to the network (Karygiannis & Owens 2002). Star topology, bus topology and ring topology are the most common used topologies for this process.

A single central hub that connects three or more computers in star topology. This topology can be used for home networks and small businesses. The star network is very useful for certain applications in which some processing must be centralized and some must be performed locally. The problem in this star topology is its susceptibility because here all data must pass through one central host and if that particular host fails, the entire network will fail (Karygiannis &Owens 2002).

In bus topology, all the computers are linked on a single cable. Here, the signals are broadcasted in all directions and special software is used to identify the type of signal which is received by the system. The benefit of this network is that there is no central hub and so if one system goes down it will not affect others and it will be able to communicate with one another (Luo *et al.* 200). The drawback of this technology is only one signal can be transmitted at a time and if two or more signals are transmitted at the same time collision will occur and the signal will fail to reach its destination.

In ring topology, each host can communicate directly with any other host and each host can process independently its own applications. A ring network forms a circular ring like structure and data are sent in only one direction and if a host fails still the data transmission can be done.

Benefits of Wired Network:

Wired Network has the following benefits which include

- The bandwidth is very high and possesses limited interference because of direct connections.
- Wired networks are more secure and they are used in many applications such as corporate LANs, school networks and hospitals.
- Ethernet cables, hubs and switches are not expensive and mostly reliable because of the continuous improvement in Ethernet technology over several decades.

Drawback of Wired Network

- The main drawback of this network is that it must be rewired every time whenever it is moved.

Wireless Networks

Wireless networks are the imperative and fastest growing in our daily life. For communication between nodes, high-frequency radio waves are utilized by the wireless network instead of wires. For enhancing their existing wired network, users and organizations can utilize this alternative or to go completely wireless. Wireless network permits devices to be shared among the neighbors without networking cable, which builds portability but decreases range. Wireless network uses infrared or radio frequency signals to share the information and resource among the devices The various types of wireless devices available today include mobile terminals, pocket size PCs, handheld PCs, laptops, cellular phone, PDAs, wireless sensors, and satellite receivers, etc.(Basagni *et al.* 2004, Baumann et al, 2007).

For communication purpose, WLAN cards, wireless adapters and access points are required in wireless devices. The reliability of wireless network is less compared to the wired network. Wired Equivalent Privacy (WEP) encryption is used by WLANs for the protection of data and to make wireless networks more secure. Mobility of wireless network is better compared to the wired networks because laptops and other computing devices can be moved around freely within the network. There are two major types of wireless networking; peer to peer or ad-hoc and infrastructure.

An ad-hoc or end-to-end network is a wireless network which incorporates number of computers and is each equipped with a wireless Network Interface Card (NIC). Every computer can communicate directly with all the other wireless computers and they have the capacity to share the files and printers, but it could not access wired LAN resources, unless one of the computers acts as a bridge to the wired LAN.

An infrastructure based wireless network consists of an access point or a base station. The access point acts like a hub in infrastructure based network to provide connectivity for the wireless computers. These networks can connect the wireless LAN to a wired LAN, permitting wireless computer access to LAN resources, such as file servers or Internet connectivity.

The Institute of Electrical and Electronic Engineers (IEEE) have produced four basic types of transmission standards that define all aspects of radio frequency for wireless networking and they include 802. , 802. a, 802. b and 802. g. The connection speed and radio frequency are the fundamental differences between these four types. 802. and 802. b will operate at the radio frequency of 2.4 GHz. But, 802. a operates at a frequency of 5 GHz and can transmit up to 54 Mbps and the 802. g operates at a frequency of 2.4 GHz and can transmit up to 54 Mbps. Based on such factors, the actual transmission speed varies inside the network.

Wireless networks are dependable compared to the wired network, yet when interruption happens, it can cut down the range and the quality of the signal. Interruption or Interference can be provided by other devices which work on the same radio frequency.

There are numerous advantages of a wireless network

- Wireless networks are far simpler to move than a wired network and also for adding users to an existing wireless network is simple.

- Wireless networks are easier for providing connectivity in region where it is hard to place cable.
- An organization can establish a wireless network without physically disturbing the present working environment or wired network.
- Wireless networks Installations are quick and simple.
- Anywhere within the range of an access point wireless network can be connected.
- Long-term cost benefits can be found in dynamic background which requires frequent moves and changes.

Need of Wireless Network

Recently, compared to wired technology, the wireless network plays the most significant task, (Capkun *et al.* 2004) for achieving the requirement of the network users. Due to its complication, wired network is more expensive when compared to the wireless network.

WIRELESS AD HOC NETWORKS

Wireless ad hoc network is a type of multi hop wireless network without using any infrastructure. Using radio signals, nodes are communicated. Due to the wireless nature, it overcomes most of the limitations of traditional wired networks (Pietro *et al.* 20 4). For better communication, the mobile nodes in the network cooperate with each other. Each mobile node operates not only as a host but also as a router that forwards packets on behalf of other nodes (Deng *et al.* 2002).

Due to the inherent characteristics of wireless ad hoc networks such as dynamic topology, limited channel capacity, power constraints, open shared medium and wireless transmission impairments, the network is more vulnerable to utilize the resources and achieves throughput. Hence, designing an effective routing protocol for ad hoc network still remains as a challenging task. The applications of ad hoc networks range from military operations, emergency disaster recovery, community networking and ad hoc interaction meeting among persons in a conference hall. Mobile Ad hoc Networks (MANET), Wireless Mesh Networks (WMN) and Wireless Sensor Networks (WSN) are classified as three types of wireless Ad hoc networks based on their applications.

WIRELESS MESH NETWORKS

A wireless technology that predominantly enjoys the widespread use of the *Wireless Local Area Network* (WLAN). The standard communication technology for WLAN is IEEE 802. (IEEE std. 802. , 999) commonly known as "Wi-Fi". Infrastructure-based WLANs which are fast replacing their wired counterparts, due to their cheap cost, flexibility, and the convenience that offer over conventional local area wired networks. They have been generally deployed at places like offices, cafes, universities and airports. Despite their extensive deployment, infrastructure-based WLANs have certain limitations, most notably the need of a wired connection to the access network (typically Ethernet) for every *Access Point* (AP). Extending the wireless coverage of a WLAN by installing multiple APs becomes costly and impractical, due to extensive cabling requirements. To overcome the limitations, *Wireless Mesh Network* (WMN) has been proposed. Mesh networks have gained enormous attention because of their capability of providing broadband wireless coverage to large areas without infrastructure requirements. The mesh network acts as a common backhaul network providing interconnection between ranges of heterogeneous networks as well as providing ultimate access to the Internet.

Wireless mesh networks are a special case of wireless multi-hop networks. They comprise a static wireless backbone without mobility or energy requirements. The nodes are interconnected wirelessly and they create a"*mesh*" of connections. The mesh routers act as wireless *Access Points* to which other users and user networks connect. A few routers in the network provide wired connection to the Internet, and these routers are called gateways. Many number of communication technologies have been proposed for mesh networking, principally, IEEE 802. (Wi-Fi) and 802. 6 (WiMax). IEEE 802. -based mesh networks remain the most popular because of cheap equipment cost and off-the-shelf availability. Mesh networks typically serve a large number of users who demand efficient performance (high end-to-end throughput, small end-to-end delay, high reliability etc). Mesh networks are mostly used in the context of providing *last-mile* access to the Internet so that, significant portions of traffic in mesh networks is between mesh routers and it connects the users and the gateway nodes. This underlying traffic pattern may result in congestion leading to poor performance in some areas of the network. Most importantly, a major performance bottleneck in 802. -based mesh networks is that a large number of mesh routers are located within the same geographical area and they share the same wireless medium which can cause strong "*interference*" between mesh routers. This results in significant performance degradation in terms of the achievable throughput and the end-to-end delays. High interference, unique traffic patterns and high performance requirements from mesh networks are mandate research for efficient routing and QoS strategies focused on mesh networks. The focus of our work is on several issues in routing and QoS of mesh networks: *efficient routing, optimal encoder node selection, enhanced route stability* and *per-flow bandwidth guarantees.*

Components of a Wireless Mesh Network

Mesh networks comprise three types of nodes: *Mesh Routers* (or Access Points - APs), *Mesh Clients* and *Gateway Routers* as shown in Figure . .

Mesh Routers maintain connectivity, perform routing and provide the wireless backbone. They form an infrastructure of wirelessly interconnected routers that provide service to the users. They usually have negligible or no mobility and are not power constrained. These routers sometimes carry multiple radio interfaces. They are similar to the conventional routers in that they have the gateway/bridging functionality, but they also have the added functionality to handle the mesh infrastructure. Instead of acting like terminal or user stations, the mesh routers act as relays to provide access to the users and the user networks connected to these mesh routers.

Mesh Client consists of end user devices such as laptops, PDAs Pocket PCs. The mesh clients can route data among themselves. The mesh clients can connect to the network either directly through the network gateways, or through the mesh routers.

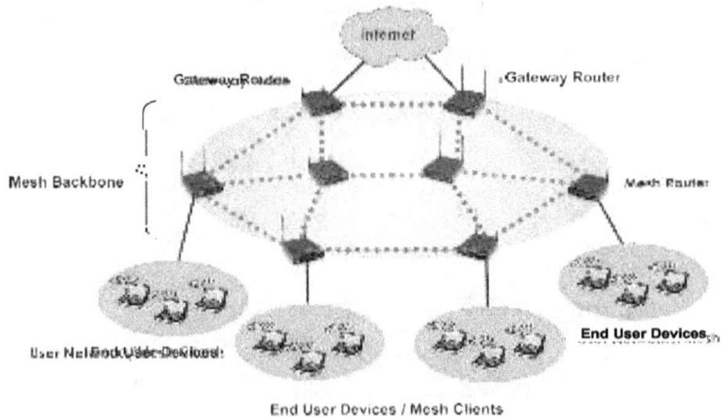

(Source: Akyildiz *et al.* 2005)

Figure 1.1 Wireless Mesh Network

Gateway Routers connect the wireless mesh network either directly to the internet or to the wired access network (typically Ethernet) which is eventually connected to the internet. Gateway routers act as the bridge between the wireless mesh domain and the wired internet domain.

Classification of Wireless Mesh Networks

Wireless mesh networks are sometimes classified as ***Backbone*** (or ***Infrastructure***) and ***Client*** mesh networks and they are also classified based on the number of radios and the number of available channels.

Backbone (or Infrastructure Wireless Mesh Networks) - The backbone mesh network consists of static wireless mesh routers that maintain connectivity, perform routing and provide the wireless backbone. These routers form an infrastructure of wirelessly interconnected routers that provide service to the users and networks. These WMN routers typically carry multiple radio interfaces for the wireless backhaul and one radio interface for connection with the end devices and networks.

Client Mesh Networks - Client mesh networks consist of a network of end- user devices such as laptops. These are self-organizing nodes that may perform routing among themselves. They give network wide services to users and may optionally be connected to a network of backbone wireless mesh routers which may or may not have a connection to the wired Internet. These devices are usually power-constrained with energy-limitations and are typically mobile.

Single-Radio Single-Channel Wireless Mesh Networks-Single-radio, single-channel network is the most basic type of wireless mesh network. Each node in the network is equipped with a single radio and radio interfaces at all nodes are tuned to the same frequency channel. Mostly, it suffers from performance problems (Gupta 2000), and the main reason being the single channel and strong interference between mesh routers. In a mesh network, a large number of routers are located in close proximity. They traditionally use the IEEE 802. communication technology which works on the principle of CSMA (*Carrier Sense Multiple Access*) where nodes contend for access to the channel and a large number of mesh routers contending for access to the same channel can create high interference.

Multi-Radio Multi-Channel Wireless Mesh Networks-Each node is equipped with one or more radios and the radio interfaces are typically tuned to non-overlapping channels to minimize interference. There are *Static Channel Assignment*, *Dynamic Channel Assignment* or a combination of the two. In *Static Channel Assignment*, the interfaces at all nodes are permanently tuned to a fixed channel to minimize interference between the routers. In contrast, *Dynamic Channel Assignment* provides a mechanism for dynamically switching the interface to a different channel, as the load conditions on the network vary. Dynamic channel assignment is more complex, as it requires some underlying channel switching algorithm, a mechanism for synchronizing channel switch and a way to handle the channel switch latency [R. Draves 04b] [A. P. Subramanian 06]. This latency occurs, due to the limitations of the currently available 802. hardware [R. Chandra 04]. A hybrid channel assignment can also be used and it is a combination of static and dynamic channel assignment. In these solutions, some of the interfaces are permanently assigned with a fixed channel (often referred to as a control channel) while other interfaces can dynamically switch channels.

Communication Technologies for Wireless Mesh Networks

The advanced two technologies that are the key candidates for providing backhaul wireless internet are *Wi-Fi* (IEEE 802. x) and *WiMax* (IEEE 802. 6x). The two technologies have totally different characteristics and offer different communication solutions. Some key differences between the two principal technologies are outlined below:

IEEE 802.11 - The most widely used communication technology for wireless mesh networks is IEEE 802. . This is mainly due to the fact that it operates in the license-free zone. A *Wi-Fi* mesh network consists of multiple 802. *Access Points* (AP) interconnected wirelessly. These nodes act as backhaul wireless mesh network to provide wireless coverage to large areas. Each AP acts as a router, accepting user connections in its locality and routing their data wirelessly over multiple hops to a wired connection and vice versa. The primary benefit of using 802. is that *off-the-shelf* 802. standard products are easily available and the technology operates in an unlicensed band. The cost of the IEEE 802. equipment is cheap and the Initial investment is therefore cost effective for small deployments. Some disadvantages of using IEEE 802. as the communication technology are the following. First, the bandwidth is shared among a large group of users. Secondly, due to limited data rate, the achievable throughput is limited and there can be significant delay and jitter. Due to the probabilistic access mechanism of IEEE 802. , providing QoS is challenging.

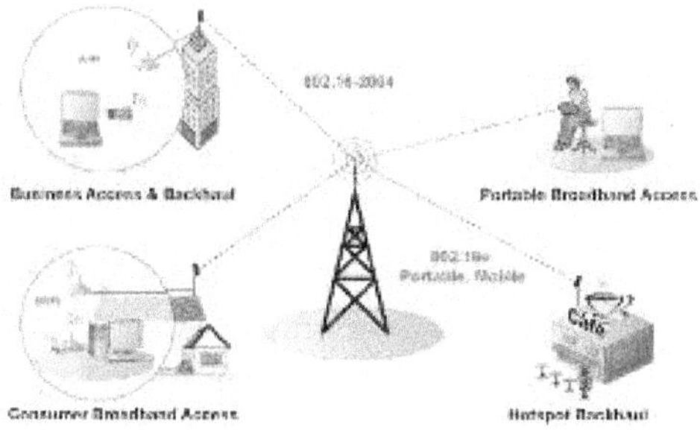

Figure 1.2 - *WiMax Network* (IEEE 802.16, 2004)

IEEE 802.16 - IEEE 802. 6 as shown in figure .2 networks are basically aimed at offering data services in a localized area e.g. a university building. The IEEE 802. 6 standard in contrast, is aimed at providing wireless broadband to metropolitan areas. During the recent years, 802. 6 has begun to be used as the communication technology for back- bone mesh networks. WiMAX (Worldwide Interoperability for Microwave Access) is the commercialization of the IEEE 802. 6 standard. Initially, the 802. 6 standard was aimed at serving fixed subscriber stations (SSs) through the central *Base Station* (BS) by using the P*oint-to-Multipoin*t (PMP) topology. However, in IEEE 802. 6, which is the current standard, an additional mode called the *mesh-mode* has been introduced. In IEEE 802. 6 *mesh-mode*, a mesh *Base Station* (BS) acts as the mesh back- bone and controls *Subscriber Stations* (SS). With the centralized scheduling scheme of mesh mode, the Mesh Base Station is responsible for managing the allocation of resources as well as collecting bandwidth requests from subscriber stations. The 802. 6 mesh provides some improvements compared to the IEEE 802. technology, but has some limitations. For example, the *mesh-mode* only defines *per-link, per-hop* QoS mechanism which is not very appropriate for broadband QoS support in an end-to-end scenario within the mesh network.

Characteristics of Wireless Mesh Network

The characteristics of WMNs are summarized below:

- WMNs are **multi-hop wireless networks** (Draves *et al.* 2004a) that perform communication through MR as a part of Infrastructure/Backbone WMNs. Since most of the networks communications are error prone and difficult to diagnoses or repair, WMNs define the backbone based communication which allows bridges among the network for communication. This allows multi-hop communication to avoid any failure (Draves *et al.* 2004b; Jain *et al.* 2005).
- WMNs are **intelligent networks** that have the capability of identifying any failure and adapt accordingly to solve the problem. WMNs are self-forming network that holds and possesses the capability to establish new network routing path in case of any failure. WMNs are also self-healing networks that automatically rectify any problem mainly by allowing multipath communication to support the systems. Above all, WMNs are self-organizing networks that can be used to connect

with wired and other network communication and thus, becomes the part of big group networks.

- WMNs have **minimal mobile routers** that provide efficient and dedicated part for the communication scenarios. Mesh routers are self-organization structures that perform dedicated routing and configuration. This significantly reduces the load of mesh clients and other end nodes, and also allow opportunistic environment for establishing communication. Mesh routers are usually minimal mobile natured system where mesh clients can be stationary or mobile nodes.
- WMNs **support mobility** (Akyildiz *et al.* 999) for the communication, since it is the backbone of the entire network communication. WMNs allow and support ad-hoc network as end nodes that can be supported easily through the wireless infrastructure. WMN support multiple networks for communication and extend self-organization among the various networks (Akyildiz *et al.* 2004; Chen & Chen 2003).
- WMNs allow **integration** among heterogeneous networks, including both wired and wireless. WMNs allow connection among multiple networks type and communicate through these network. Access of multiple types of network exists in WMNs. Mesh connectivity provides many advantages to WMNs origination. To ensure reliable mesh connectivity, there is a need of network self-organization and topology control algorithms. Topology-aware Medium Access Control (MAC) and routing protocols can significantly improve the performance of WMNs (Bellofiore *et al.* 2002).

- WMNs have **constrained power-consumption** (Bhatia & Kodialam 2004) that is defined based on the capabilities and usage of different tasks for different mesh routers and mesh clients. The power consumption of WMNs is based on the requirement and usage of the systems (Chiasserini & Rao 2000). WMNs act as a backbone for the connectivity of various networks. Hence, the power consumption of the system is dependent on the type of application. However, mesh clients may require power efficient protocols. As an example, a mesh-capable sensor (Grilo & Nunes 2003) requires its communication protocols to be power efficient.
- WMNs provide **compatibility and inter-operability**. WMNs are not stand-alone networks rather they need to be compatible and interoperable with other wireless networks. WMNs do not provide straight operation but act as the back bone of the communication network. Inter-operability among the network is allowed and thus allows communication efficiently.
- WMNs are **easy to handle** and simple to utilize. Protocols assigned and used in the network are designed to enable the network to be autonomous as possible. WMNs are compatible with multiple networks and thus, require efficient protocol for stable and effective communication.

Therefore, WMNs provide diversified systems which possess the capabilities of ad-hoc networks in spite of being another type of ad-hoc network. These extra capabilities require and necessitate for the new algorithms and design principles for the realization of WMNs.

Comparison of Ad Hoc and Wireless Mesh Network

The fundamental differences of wireless mesh networks compared to Mobile Ad-hoc Networks(MANET) are listed below(Yan Zhang *et al.* 2006):

WMNs are relatively static based on the network topology and wireless ad-hoc networks are highly dynamic in nature. In WMNs, the mobility of the relay nodes and energy constraints are low whereas MANET has medium or high mobility and energy constraints. WMNs are connected with partial or full infrastructure based network where the MANET is an infrastructure less network.

The routing performance of WMN is fully or partially distributed with the preference of table driven or hierarchical routing but mobile ad-hoc networks have the preference of fully distributed on-demand routing. The WMNs relay on fixed as well as mobile nodes wherever the mobile ad-hoc network relies only on mobile nodes.

Advantages of Wireless Mesh Networks

Self-Organizing and Self-Configuring - Wireless mesh networks are self-configuring and in general, nodes can be added and removed from the network when needed without any special administrative intervention. The nodes in a WMN learn about their neighbors and dynamically route data among themselves. Nodes enter and leave the network, some connections fail, and new connections are created. All there are handled by the mesh routing protocol.

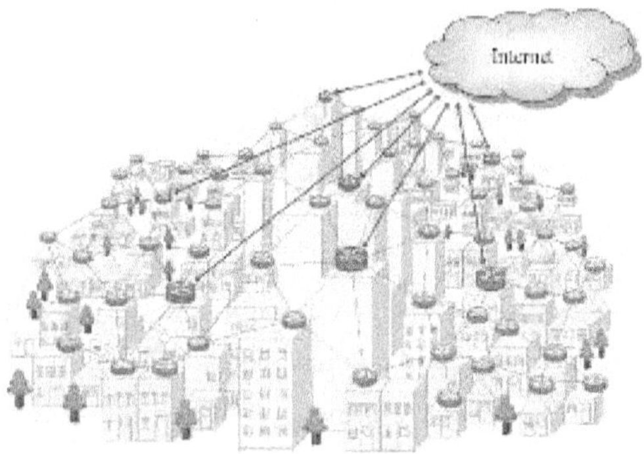

(Source: Hamid Hamraz &Golnar Bidkhori 2011)

Figure 1.3 Mesh network spanning a complete city

Self-Healing - Wireless mesh networks are self-healing in that the failing of some nodes or routes does not necessarily require administrative intervention or disruption of service. In fact, the term "*mesh*" means that the nodes are "*meshed*" together and there exists a number of alternate routes when some routes fail. Self-healing capability also depends on the degree of "*meshing*" which implies the number of alternate available routes.

Rapid Deployment - Compared to the traditional infrastructure-based wireless networks, mesh networks are relatively easy to deploy. The principle difference stems from the fact that WLANs require wired connections of APs to the wired access network. However, mesh nodes can be quickly deployed, as they do not have strict architectural constraints.

Coverage Extension and Scalability - The range of a wireless mesh network can be significantly extended to cover large areas (Figure .3) using the multi-hop routing capability. Nodes can be easily added when required to expand the coverage. In contrast, conventional wireless networks such as WLANs have scalability problems due to the requirement of wired connection for every Access Point. Therefore, WLANs are typically limited to small building or area. Real-world mesh networks as large as up to 800 nodes and spanning several miles [Fre 09] have been successfully deployed in real world environments. In general, mesh networks can easily be scaled to cover large geographical areas.

Application Scenarios of WMNS

Wireless Mesh Networks are constructed in many places based on the applications like emergency situations, tunnels, oil rigs, battlefield surveillance, and high speed mobile video applications on board public transport or real time racing car telemetry, Health and medical systems. By using a Quality of Service scheme, the wireless mesh may support local telephone calls to be routed through the mesh.

ROUTING IN WIRELESS MESH NETWORK

Routing is the progression of discovering the end to end path from source node to destination node. Routing protocols are the heart of multi-hop wireless networks, as they control the creation, configuration and maintenance of the topology of the network (Siva Nageswara Rao *et al.* 20). Routing protocols in wireless networks can be classified as proactive, reactive and hybrid (hierarchical) routing protocols. Since WMNs share the common features with ad hoc networks, the routing protocols designed for ad hoc networks can be incorporated in WMNs with essential modifications.

Proactive Routing Protocols

The routing paths are discovered here are regardless of the readiness of a node to transmit data. Routing tables are maintained at each node and the discovered routes are stored in the tables. Whenever a node wants to transmit data, it refers to the routing table. If the required path is available, it utilizes the path information to transmit data. Otherwise, it initiates the route discovery process. Periodically the routing information is exchanged among the nodes and stored in the routing tables at each node. Hence, these protocols suffer from high amount of control packets overhead and more power consumption even there exists no data transmission in the network. Optimized Link State Routing (OLSR) and Destination Sequenced Distance Vector (DSDV) routing protocols are the most popularly used proactive routing protocols.

Optimized Link State Routing (Clausen & Jacquet 2003) is an optimized version of link state algorithm designed for ad hoc network. It is a proactive routing protocol and thus, routes are always available in the routing table (Modassir Ishfaq 20 4). The aim is to minimize duplicate retransmissions in the same area. All nodes in the network exchange routing information periodically to maintain topology updates. Multi Point Relay (MPR) selectors are unique to OLSR so that, nodes selected as MPRs only forward control packets thereby, control overhead substantially is reduced. Each node broadcasts hello packets periodically to search next hop neighbours, MPR selection process and also for link sensing. Every node can get topology information up to two hops from the hello packets and thus, used for calculating MPR set. Every node maintains MPR selector table where nodes selected as MPRs are recorded and updated periodically. Hence, each node broadcasts only its MPR selector information rather than broadcasting the whole neighbour information. Intermediate nodes, by receiving the MPR information, recalculate and update the routes to the known destinations.

Destination Sequenced Distance Vector Routing Protocol (Perkins & Bhagwat 994) is a proactive routing protocol which is designed based on the traditional Bellman Ford algorithm. Sequence numbers are used in DSDV routing protocol to avoid the formation of routing loops. At every node, routing table is maintained and it stores next hop information towards a destination, cost metric for a path to the destination node and a destination sequence number. Periodically, each node transmits the updated routing information to its neighbour nodes. In this protocol, the route with highest sequence number is selected for packet transmission (Liu et al. 2008).

Reactive Routing Protocols

Reactive Routing Protocols are also known as on-demand routing protocols where route discovery process is initiated whenever a node wants to transmit data to some other node. Even though, the overhead caused by the control packets occur only on demand, it requires additional latency for route discovery before the data are delivered. In these schemes, nodes maintain routes to active destinations in their routing tables. For unknown destination node, a new route discovery process should be initiated. Ad hoc On-Demand Distance Vector (AODV) routing protocol and Dynamic Source Routing (DSR) protocol are two commonly used reactive routing protocols designed for ad hoc networks (Modassir Ishfaq 20 4). AOMDV (Ad-hoc On-Demand Multipath Distance Vector) (Marina & Das 200) is an another on- demand multipath reactive routing protocol. It provides better fault tolerance by discovering multiple link disjoint and loop free paths from source to destination.

Dynamic Source Routing (David *et al.* 2007) is a popular reactive source routing protocol where route discovery and maintenance processes are initiated on demand and source routing algorithm is implemented. In DSR, each data packet contains complete routing information to reach the destination. The major phases in DSR are route discovery and route maintenance. During route discovery, each node broadcasts a Route Request (RREQ) packet along with its source routing table. Upon receiving the RREQ message, each intermediate node appends its own identifier to the routing table in the routing message and forwards to its neighbor nodes. For every intermediate node, it is repeated until it reaches the destination and then, destination unicast Route Reply (RREP) packet to the source node. DSR incurs additional overhead, since data packets carry the entire routing information during the hop by hop transmission which degrades the network performance (Liu *et al.* 2008).

Adhoc on-demand Distance Vector (AODV) (Perkins & Royer 999) is an another familiar reactive on demand routing protocol designed for mobile ad hoc networks and it is based on both DSDV and DSR. Hence, it owns the advantages of both protocols like keeping the track of destination sequence number to avoid routing loops etc. Contrast to these two protocols, in AODV, each node has to maintain only the routing information about the source, destination and next hop information which in turn minimizes the traffic overhead. Route discovery process in AODV is designed as same as DSR by broadcasting RREQ control packets. An intermediate node or the destination node unicast RREP control packet, when active route is found (Liu *et al.* 2008).

Hybrid Routing Protocols

Hybrid routing protocols are the combination of table driven and reactive routing protocols and thus take the advantages of the best features of both types. The aim is to reduce the control overhead occurring in proactive routing approaches and to minimize the delay caused for reactive route discovery approaches. Nodes which are available within the particular geographical area in the network belong to a common routing zone and proactive routing protocol is used in that zone. For nodes which are located outside the zone, route discovery is performed in a reactive way. Hence in hybrid routing protocols, route discovery takes place by using both proactive and reactive routing approaches. These protocols are also classified based on zonal and convergence characteristics. Zonal Routing Protocol (ZRP) is the hybrid routing protocol designed for ad hoc networks where both proactive and reactive routing protocols are implemented at different network areas. In convergence approaches, on- demand mechanisms are needed to change the protocol functionality from proactive to reactive or vice versa.

Zonal Routing Protocol is a hybrid wireless networking protocol proposed by Haas *et al.* (998) to speed up the packet delivery process and to minimize the control overhead by making use of both proactive and reactive routing approaches. For each node in the ad hoc network, a routing zone is defined separately. Nodes, which are within the same routing zone, can use proactive routing approach. For nodes outside the zone, route discovery is initiated by using an on demand approach. ZRP uses two sub routing protocols namely Intra-zone Routing Protocol (IARP) which is proactive and is used within the routing zone. The other one is Inter-zone Routing Protocol (IERP) which is reactive and is used between the routing zones.

Cross - layer Routing Protocols

In order to improve the performance, recently there has been an increasing interest in protocols which use interaction between different layers of the protocol stack. Traditionally, a layered approach to routing was adopted in order to keep things compartmentalized, but recent research has shown that at the cost of breaking the traditional layered structure, significant performance gains can be achieved. Cross-layered routing solutions particularly aim at the interaction of lower layers with the network layer. The argument is that the channel information available at the lower layers, particularly the Physical layer, is more accurate and using this information at the higher layers to make routing decisions, significant performance improvements can be provided. Recently, cross-layer solutions have been proposed for wireless mesh networks

(Iannone *et al.* 2005). The counter argument against such approaches is that while performance gains do provide a certain motivation, breaking the layered architecture means that it will be difficult to have vendors adopt the solution.

In this thesis work, the routing protocols which are designed based on reactive routing approach have been proposed. Route discovery process is carried out on demand by any node (source) by broadcasting Route Request (RREQ) packets and destination node unicasts a Route Reply (RREP) packet to the source node. The routing fields in RREQ and RREP packet are modified according to the security and performance enhancements are made in the proposed approach. Destination node receives RREQ packets through multiple routing paths and it selects an optimal routing path through which RREP packet is unicasted.

Design Considerations for Routing Protocols in Mesh Networks

Routing in wireless mesh networks differs significantly from the wired networks or the conventional ad hoc networks. In WMNs, there are no mobility requirements or energy constraints. Routing protocols that have been proposed for adhoc networks such as MANETs and WSNs need to be improved and new protocols must be proposed that cater for the unique architecture and characteristics of the WMNs. While designing routing protocols, many design options are available at various levels. In the context of Wireless Mesh Networks, the following criteria are considered for classifying and evaluating routing protocols.

Type of Protocol: An important classification in routing protocols is whether they are proactive or reactive. The obvious strength of a proactive routing scheme is that routes are available when needed, but the disadvantage is the overhead associated with the periodic refreshing of messages. The advantage of a reactive routing scheme is the small routing overhead, but it introduces delays in communication because the routes are not immediately available. A third type of routing protocol also exists and that is a mix of the above two types. It is called hybrid routing. In some scenarios, hybrid protocols are the most promising approach, as they can combine the strengths of the two types. Choosing a correct protocol depends heavily on the network scenario in which routing will take place.

Base Protocol: Quite some researchers have been done on routing protocols in ad hoc networks and several efficient and rigorously tested protocols have been proposed. Since WMNs are a type of ad hoc networks therefore, the protocols for ad hoc networks have received much attention of the researchers. Many of the protocols suggested for WMNs have their roots in these protocols such as SrcRR (Aguayo 05), AODV-MR (Pirzada *et al.* 2007), AODV-ST (Ramachandran 05a). Thus, routing protocols for these networks can be developed by basing them on some existing protocols.

Network Structure: Routing in infrastructure mesh networks differs significantly from routing in the backbone mesh. This is primarily because the client nodes are usually mobile and will be generally battery constrained while the backbone mesh network has no mobility or energy constraints. Thus, while developing the protocol for WMNs, it must be kept in mind that which type of infrastructure is targeted.

Radio Interfaces and Channels: Currently, the most common type of mesh networks is the single-radio because of the simplicity of architecture and cheap cost. Using multiple radio interfaces over non-overlapping channels, the capacity of the network can be significantly improved and another performance can be improved by reducing interference. It is a design parameter to consider whether the protocol being developed will be used for single-radio, single-channel mesh networks or multi-radio multi-channel mesh networks. The design principles of the protocol will differ significantly for the different architectures.

Protocol Structure: Conventionally, the protocol stack is a structured entity with clear separation between different layers of the stack. Interaction among the layers takes place across well defined interfaces. This ensures that the changes and improvements can be made in one layer without worrying about the other layers. Due to the peculiar characteristics of the wireless mesh networks, sometimes the conventional layering does not yield the optimal approach. The down multiple layers have to be melt into one layer in order to fully exploit the channel characteristics of the WMNs. Some works suggest that improvements in capacity throughput can be achieved by adopting a cross-layering approach. Thus, choosing to stay with the conventional structured routing structure or adopting a cross layered approach is an another important design decision.

Underlying MAC protocol: Some routing protocols are MAC independent while others rely heavily on the type of MAC layer. Two broad classes of MAC protocols are: TDMA based MAC and CSMA based MAC. The routing solutions of these two classes of protocols will differ significantly.

Routing Protocols in Wireless Mesh Networks

Lot of routing protocols have been proposed for Wireless mesh networks. A flavor of the different approaches adopted by researchers has been described.

SrcRR: The SrcRR protocol (Aguayo *et al.* 2005) is used by the Roofnet mesh testbed at MIT. The initial routing protocol used in the test-bed was DSR with Expected Transmission Count - ETX [De Couto 03] as the routing metric. For bulk TCP transfers, the protocol performed quite poorly and so the authors proposed an optimized version of the DSR called SrcRR. The SrcRR protocol is a reactive protocol with source-routed traffic. Every node running SrcRR maintains a link cache in which it has ETX metric values for links about which it has heard recently. SrcRR improves on DSR with ETX in many ways. It improves route stability by making less frequent changes and prefers using the same route as long as the new route offers only slight improvement. It also avoids discarding packets immediately, due to link-level transmission failures. It retries persistently to avoid TCP time-outs and the resulting under-utilization. With all these improvements, the authors have shown a significant increase in the TCP throughput.

LQSR: Link Quality State Routing protocol [padhye et al,2004] is based on the DSR protocol. It is a link-state protocol with source-routed data. LQSR uses the Expected Transmission Time (ETT) routing metric which is the expected time to transmit a fixed-size packet on a particular link. The MR-LQSR (Draves et al ,2004] is an extension of the LQSR protocol. It is a reactive, source-routed and link-state routing protocol derived from DSR and uses WCETT as link quality metric. It is an extension of the LQSR to handle multiple radio interfaces per node, and it yields better results. The ETT metric used by the LQSR only considers the loss-rates of the paths and does not cater for their bandwidths as well as it does not give any preference to channel diverse paths. Thus, the LQSR protocol is modified to handle multiple radio interfaces per node and it, uses more sophisticated metrics in the decision for path selection.

AODV-ST: The AODV-Spanning Tree routing protocol (Ramachandran *et al.* 2005) has been proposed in the context of a framework for routing in mesh networks. It is a routing protocol for infrastructure wireless mesh networks. The authors define the architecture as it comprises relay and gateway nodes. The relay nodes act as Access Points and provide access to the client nodes. The relay nodes interconnect wirelessly to form a self-configuring, managed and secure wireless backbone that transfers packets. The relay nodes consist of two types of interfaces: access and relay. The gateway nodes consist of relay and backhaul interfaces. The access interfaces are used to provide service to clients whereas the relay interfaces are used for relaying packets between the relay nodes. The backhaul interfaces at the gateway nodes are used to connect the internet. The AODV-ST is a reactive protocol which uses the Expected Transmission Time (ETT) metric. AODV-ST improves AODV in many ways. AODV-ST allows the use of high throughput metrics like ETT instead of the sub-optimal hop-count metric used by AODV. It allows the pro-active maintenance of Spanning Trees whose roots are the gateway nodes, thus reduces route discover latency and improves performance. It also reduces the size of routing tables maintained at nodes.

MRS: The Mesh Routing Strategy (Iannone *et al.* 2005) is a routing solution for WMNs. It sets apart from the other routing solutions proposed in that, it uses a cross-layering approach. The authors argue that the main limiting factor in routing performance is that interference that each packet transmission generates for the surrounding nodes. The main approach here is to control the power used in transmissions at the physical layer so as to minimize interference. The protocol uses physical layer level metrics such as rate interference and Packet Error Rate (PER). The rate is the raw rate that the wireless card can send over the channel. The interference caused is estimated locally. The PER is the packet losses on the physical channel.

HWMP (IEEE *802.11*s Standard): The upcoming IEEE 802. s draft standard proposes the Hybrid Wireless Mesh Protocol (HWMP) as the default routing protocol for mesh networks. HWMP uses a proactive routing approach for gateway discovery in mesh networks. Gateways periodically broadcast special Route Request packets which are flooded throughout the network and mesh routers select the best gateway based upon a routing metric. Within the mesh network itself, the standard proposes an on-demand routing protocol (based on AODV) to find the routes between mesh peers. While 802. s proposes using the Airtime metric for routing within the mesh network, the choice of a routing metric for gateway selection is left open.

NETWORK CODING

Increased number of packet transmission in Multihop communication reduces the network throughput capacity in wireless mesh networks. In the past decade, numerous methods such as multi-channel transmission through NICs (multiple network interface cards), multi-path transmission and network-coding were employed to improve the throughput of WMNs.

Network coding is referred to as the coding done at node in a packet network with error free links. It is a method of encoding and decoding the transmitted data for the intension of increasing the throughput, reducing the delay there by obtaining robust mesh network and it has been widely used in much type of networks i.e. conventional wireless network, wireless sensor network, video multicast network, peer to peer network etc., (Guo *et al.* 20). In network coding, the intermediate node or router in the network can mix the incoming packets as long as destination node is able to recover the original packet instead of forwarding the same content sent by source node (Sengupta *et al.* 2007). Traditionally, a network delivers information using the store and forward technique. On the other hand, network coding technique breaks this tradition and allows nodes in a network not only to store and forward but also intelligently combine and compute the independent in-coming information flows into an outgoing flow and hence, it improves the reliability. The network-coding has been considered as a recently emerged 'coding paradigm' which can be effectively employed to enhance the throughput performance of Wireless Mesh Networks (WMNs). In this work, the low network throughput problem faced in WMNs has been tackled using network-coding.

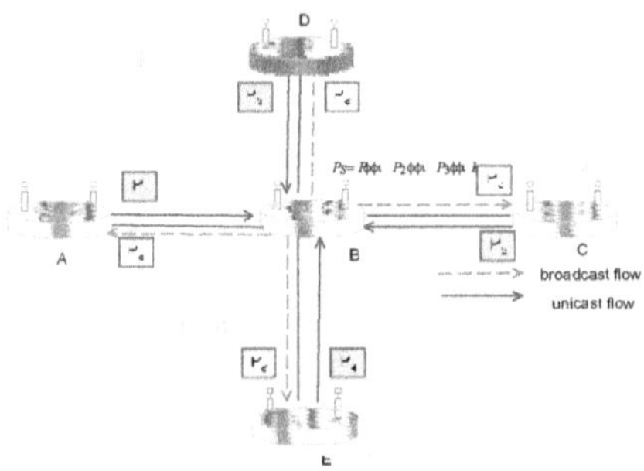

Figure 1.4 Example for Network-coding

The throughput advantage attained using network-coding techniques is explained below with an example. Figure .4 depicts the four different types of anticipated (intended) packet transmissions such as i) packet $P$from node F to H; ii) packet P_2 from node H to F; iii) packet P_3 from node I to J; and iv) packet P_4 from node J to I. But, it should be noted that node G is highly responsible to transfer these four packets. Hence, this occurs because of limited transmission range. However, following the conventional "store-and-forward" routing technique, packet transmission occurs twice a time to reach its respective destination (i.e. each packet must be forwarded twice from its source to its destination). Therefore to perform these four packet transfers (exchanges), the conventional "store-and-forward" routing technique requires 8 transmissions. While in network-coding, it is assumed that the nodes such as F, H, I and J are responsible to transmit their packets serially to the 'intermediate' node G. The node F while transmitting its packets to node G (i.e. the -hop neighbors), the nodes in the 'promiscuous' mode such as, I and J will be able to 'overhear' these packets. Likewise, the packets transmitted by the node I to node G can be captured by the nodes F and H. Consequently, after completing these 4 transmissions, about 4 native-packets such as, P, P_2, P_3 and P_4 have been received by the node G in its 'local' buffer. Then, the XOR operation is employed by the node G to encode the packets P, P_2, P_3 and P_4 and as a result, the encoded packet P_S is generated. At last, this encoded packet P_S is broadcasted by the node G. Besides, the copy of the transmitted packet is still stored in each node. Like this, by employing the XOR operation in the Packets P, P_2, P_3 and P_4 with P_S (i.e. $P_S = P \mathrm{E8}\, P_2 \mathrm{E8}\, P_3 \mathrm{E8}\, P_4$) ,the node F will be able to obtain its 'desired' packet P_2. Similarly, the desired packets such as P, P_4 , and P_3 are all decoded by the nodes H, I and J. More importantly, the network-coding employed in this case, can minimize the number of transmissions (i.e. the packet exchanges can be completed with 5 packet transmissions instead of 8 in the conventional store and forward method). Thus, it is ensured that by applying the network-coding technique, the throughput is highly improved.

Lot of researches have been carried out on network coding theory. Among them, some successful categorizes of network coding schemes are XOR based network coding, linear network coding, random linear network coding and distributed random linear network coding(Sengupta et al 20 0).

NETWORK CODING SCHEMES

This thesis considers network layer network coding, which concerns the data transmission in the packet level. There are several classes of network layer network coding schemes, which are explained in the following

XOR based network coding

In the XOR based network coding schemes, bitwise XOR is performed among all or a certain set of packets at a node. XOR coding has drawn an increasing attention, due to its simplicity in both encoding and decoding processes. XOR coding is applied in COPE (Katti et.al.2008), which is the practical network coding scheme for wireless mesh networks. In COPE, each encoded packet can be decoded upon arriving at a node. In order to realize this, a router encodes packets with the assistance of MAC layer feedback information. By applying COPE, the throughput of the network can be improved.

Linear Network Coding

Linear network coding has been proved to achieve the capacity limit from the source to each receiving node in multicast networks. The capacity limit is given by max-flow min-cut bound in graph theory. More specifically, the information can be delivered from a source to a destination through the network at a maximum rate equal to the min-cut between them (Ahlswede et al. 2000). The data transmission using linear network coding scheme is specified in a multicast model, where a source multicasts to multiple receivers. Finally, at a destination node, the information of the source can be retrieved from the received packets with the aid of the channel vectors (Li *et al.* 2003). Following this, Koetter & Medard (2003) have solved an important problem of finding the encoding functions at intermediate nodes, where the encoding functions are used to determine the vectors assigned to each channel. The basic idea in this is to match the network coding solution with a solution of a set of linear equations, because every solvable multicast network has a scalar linear solution over a sufficiently large finite-field alphabet. However, linear network coding is not suitable for changing topologies because they don't have linear solutions in any field (Dougherty *et al.* 2005).

Random Linear Network Coding

To overcome the above limitations of linear network coding, Random linear network coding is proposed for unknown and changing topologies (Ho *et al.* 2006). Unlike linear network coding where every link is assigned with a planned and deterministic vector, random linear network coding enables nodes to randomly select a coefficient for each incoming packet over a finite field. The encoding functions, which determine the coefficients of the channels are required to be delivered to the destination nodes to allow them, retrieve the coded packets. Then, at a receiver, decoding can be performed by Gaussian elimination when enough number of linear independent coded packets is received. It is worth noting that the probability to achieve the theoretical multicast capacity has been exponentially approaching one with regard to the field size.

Distributed Random Linear Network Coding

In linear and random linear network coding, the global knowledge of coding coefficients is required for decoding. However, it can be difficult to achieve in reality. To solve this problem, a distributed network coding scheme has been proposed [Chou et.al. 2003]. In this, a data-aided transmission scheme is applied, where each outgoing data packet flowing on an edge of the network includes a packet header containing the coefficients of the linear combination of the coded packets. With the cost of overhead, network coding can be utilized in a decentralized manner in networks. Moreover, a generation tag is introduced to mark the coded packets that are related to the same set of source information. This method solves the problem of synchronization of incoming and outgoing packets belonging to the same set of packets. However, these methods not only increase the time complexity of network coding-based approaches, but also increase the complexity to implement them practically.

CHALLENGES IN CODE DESIGN

There are some challenges existing in the design of network coding schemes and they are summarized as follows. The XOR based coding schemes have the advantage of low computational complexity in both encoding and decoding processes (Nistor *et al.* 20) where both processes require only XOR operations. However, decoding ability of the coded packets should be taken into account in the XOR based network coding. An improper design of XOR coding may bring negative effect to a network. In some cases, a decoding may not be able to process because of lack of native packets. Therefore, decoding delay may be introduced in order to collect a native packet or it may even fail, if packets can only be sent in these coded versions. In addition, the number of native packets to be encoded affects the encoding and decoding delay because enough packets are required to be obtained before coding proceeded.

In order to apply the linear network coding in a network, several strict conditions have to be satisfied. First of all, the channels in the network have to be fixed with error free. Secondly, each channel is assigned with a vector, and the vector assigned to the outgoing channel of a node is a linear combination of the vectors assigned to its incoming channels. Thirdly, central knowledge of these vectors and network topology are required. However, real channels have errors and changing topology. Additionally, this coding scheme is ineffective in some cases (e.g., multi-source, multi-sink with arbitrary demands), because there may not exist a method to assign every channel with a coefficient satisfying the rule described above (Dougherty *et al.* 2005). Therefore, liner network coding is mostly used for theoretical analysis and it is hardly applied to real networks.

The random linear network coding schemes (Ho et al. 2006) can work in a decentralized manner and in real channels with errors. However, there are several parameters and they should be carefully designed depending on the requirements of each system that it is applied to. An important parameter is the number of packets to be encoded into a coded packet. It affects both throughput and the decoding delay. More specifically, the more packets being encoded into one coded packet, the larger throughput and longer delay the system will have. Therefore, in order to obtain higher throughput, more packets should be encoded into one coded packet. On the other hand, if packets are delay sensitive, fewer packets should be encoded into one coded packet. Yet another parameter is the size of the finite field for the coefficients. It affects the decoding probability and the size of the overhead. The larger the finite field is, the more likely that the coded packets are linearly independent and therefore, more likely to be decoded. However, the corresponding overhead and bandwidth used for transmitting these coefficients are larger.

PROBLEM SPECIFICATION

In the coding-aware routing protocol design, there are three essential aspects:) coding condition, which is used to effectively discover the coding opportunities 2) routing metric, which should carefully be designed to facilitate the routing protocol in a simple effective manner and 3) The choice of determining the forwarding list and forwarding encoder node. To circumvent all these issues mentioned above, this proposed work helps to address the above issues using any path routing (Jain & Das 2008; Dubois *et al.* 2007, Rafael Laufer & Leonard Kleinrock 20 2) and estimation of bandwidth (Surjeet *et al.* 20 4) with network coding to compute the gain of opportunistic transmission. To resolve the decision of which nodes should be included in the forwarding list for sending the encoded packet among all the intersecting nodes to obtain the highest throughput gain, most of the researchers considered the first intersecting node as an encoding node among all the intermediate nodes in wireless mesh networks, in spite of the quality of the first node. The major intention of this work is to consider delay and anypath cost metric in the routing path when deciding the encoding node in the opportunistic routing. Distributed Coding Aware Routing algorithm (DCAR) and High throughput Coding-aware Opportunistic Routing algorithm (HCOR) for wireless mesh networks exist only for single coding node along a path in the network. It is essential to design a routing algorithm that exists when multiple coding node present in the network.

Network-coding combines all the packets based on the coding strategies to save the bandwidth. It should be noted that, the packets are combined only if the coding strategies are satisfied. Also, to enjoy the whole goodness of network-coding technique, it is important to increase the quantity of coding-opportunities. To be safe from the packet loss, the incorrect packet encodings should be avoided and to support large number of packet encodings. It is essential to guarantee that the 'coding strategies' employed are necessary and correct. To override these difficulties, an improved set of coding strategies has been developed to identify large number of 'coding structures' and to support more 'packet encodings'. It is essential to design a novel routing protocol to discover the path with more benefits riding on current network traffic patterns by utilizing the proposed coding conditions.

OBJECTIVE OF RESEARCH

The prime objectives of this dissertation are

- To develop an Optimal Encoder Selection (OES) algorithm to select the optimized encode node among all the possible encoding nodes in the routing path.

2. To design an Opportunity Encoder Based Delay Aware Routing(OEDAR) algorithm for wireless mesh network using anypath cost

3. To propose an Adaptive Coding Aware Routing protocol (ACAR) to encode the packets in two different flows without the intermediate nodes in wireless mesh networks.

4. To develop a high throughput Network Coding Aware Routing (Net-CART) protocol for wireless mesh networks.

THESIS CONTRIBUTIONS

Opportunity Encoder based Delay Aware Routing (OEDAR) Algorithm in WMN

A new distributed routing algorithm OEDAR has been designed using anypath routing cost in which each node performs the coding opportunity and chooses the appropriate route by itself using the information obtained from its neighbors and the feedback from intersecting nodes in its routes. OEDAR intents to resolve whether the network coding is supposed to be done based on the coding conditions and which nodes ought to be used as the encoding nodes to obtain highest throughput gain. To realize OEDAR, every encoded node within two hop regions will get selected and also each node performs the computation of temporary anypath cost and total delay independently for each encoded flow using Optimal Encoder Selection (OES) algorithm. Anypath routing cost is computed from Expected Transmission Count (ETX) and weighted average cost of the node. All flows constantly choose the lowest anypath cost path and minimal delay as their transmission route. Some opportunistic overhearing may be failed, owing to the channel fading or packet collision at the link layer. Because of that, neighboring nodes with high probability of overhearing (> 0.8) in the coding judgment have been chosen in OEDAR. Prior to network coding, the coding node must ensure whether the encoded flow is decodable which means at least one node in the backward list is able to decode this encoded flow. To ensure this, the coding node must have the decoding knowledge before taking any coding decision. OEDAR is able to handle diverse environments, such as multiple flow rates and multiple coding nodes along the route. The performance is studied with various routing parameters such us delay, throughput and packet delivery ratio compared to the existing High throughput Coding-aware Opportunistic Routing algorithm (HCOR) in wireless mesh networks.

Adaptive Coding Aware Routing Algorithm in Wireless Mesh Networks with Multiple QOS Constraints (ACAR)

A new improved Adaptive Coding Aware Routing algorithm (ACAR) has been designed by considering anypath routing cost, delay and bandwidth of selected flow. This study also establishes and observes a optimal encoder node for two distinct flows that will not have the intermediate node in wireless mesh networks. The proposed encoder node selection algorithm is projected to improve the performance of routing protocol for the transmission of packets in wireless mesh networks. Among all possible paths, the anypath is selected based on the shortest Expected Transmission Count (ETX). In any path routing, an intermediate node receives a packet from a flow only when the destination and neighbors should be in the downstream of this flow. According to the Adaptive optimal encoder coding condition in ACAR algorithm, the potential decoding nodes of this packet should be either in destination or in one hop before destination. ACAR algorithm is applied, when two flows don't have the intermediate node but have the common overhearing node for any one of the flow. S-ACAR algorithm is applicable only when two flows have common overhearing node in the network. Then any one of the optimal node is selected and it should be placed in neighbor list of two flows. It should satisfy the coding condition i.e. destination of flow A should be listed in forwarder list of flow B and destination of flow B should be listed in forwarder list of flow A. The performance results of this ACAR gives better results by improving the average throughput and packet delivery ratio and also reducing delay consumption with increasing nodes compared to the existing protocol.

Net-CART: Modeling a Novel Network Coding Aware Routing Protocol for Enhancement of Network Performance in Wireless Mesh Network

A proposed Network Coding Aware Routing (Net-CART) protocol in wireless mesh networks considers the scenario that more than two flows intersect at one node. An improved set of coding strategies called Enhanced Universal Coding strategies (EUCS) is also proposed to determine large number of coding opportunities. A node in the Net-CART approach adapts the EUCS to find whether the packets can be 'encoded' collectively or not. Beyond this newly developed coding strategies a new metric, Code-Aware and Load-Aware Route Metric (CALARM) has been developed to utilize the whole goodness of network coding and to enhance the network throughput. CALARM is modeled based on small amount of transmission and the coding opportunities are considered to transmit a packet from source to its respective destination. The path with minimum CALARM value requires minimum number of transmissions to send a packet from the source to its respective destination. Hence, the source node selects the optimal path for packet transmission. A new control packet RvRoup (Reverse-Route-Update) is employed to compute the CALARM value of a path easily and it is updated periodically. Using this RvRoup method, a source node receives the latest information about the network and also based on the CALARM routing metric, the source node selects the most ideal path for transmission of packets. Following the basics of

Dynamic Source Routing (DSR) and FORM protocol, the Net-CART has been proposed for perfect transmission of packets to the destination.

ORGANIZATION OF THE THESIS

This dissertation has been organized into seven chapters

Chapter 1 describes the introduction about the mesh networks and Network coding technique. Also this section points out the types of network coding algorithms and route metrics used in networks.

Chapter 2 reviews earlier efforts made by various researchers in the field of the network coding framework based on quality of service concepts. Methods for computing the anypath cost, delay and estimated bandwidth are also discussed.

Chapter 3, a novel coding-aware opportunistic routing scheme OEDAR has been proposed to learn the characteristic of employing network coding into opportunistic routing there by figuring out some conclusions for designing a coding-aware opportunistic routing. Potential and optimal coding has been utilized for the consideration of route selection in OEDAR to prove the effectiveness of the system.

Chapter 4 presents methods of the second framework of the dissertation wherein Adaptive Coding Aware Routing protocols (ACAR), to encode the packets in two different flows will not have the intermediate nodes. F-ACAR protocol selects the optimal and adaptive encoder node from any one of the distinct flows and S-ACAR selects encoding node which will be the neighboring of the forwarding nodes of two distinct flows based on the anypath cost, delay and bandwidth estimation metrics. Implementation and evaluation of the second proposed framework are also portrayed.

Chapter 5 deals with a Network Coding Aware Routing (Net-CART) protocol for wireless mesh networks. It uses a coding-aware and load-aware routing metric (CALARM) to take the full advantage of the network coding benefit. An improved set of coding conditions called Enhanced Universal Coding Conditions (EUCC) is also discussed to find more coding structures and to encourage more packet encodings.

Chapter 6 describes the comparisons that are performed to assess the analysis of the proposed frameworks in terms of throughput, packet delivery ratio and delay.

Chapter 7 reveals the conclusion and summary of the proposed works.

CHAPTER 2

LITERATURE REVIEW

This chapter summarizes the routing protocol and algorithm used in WMNs. It also discusses the routing metrics used in WMNs and network coding to improve the performance of the proposed system. The routing protocol should concern with QoS by selecting the best route depending on the traffic type. A detailed review of literature related to the present work is also presented. The review has been presented under the following topics.

i. Hop-count based Routing schemes in WMN

ii. Opportunistic Routing in WMN

iii. Routing Metrics for Wireless Mesh Networks

iv. Routing towards throughput and end-end delay improvement

v. Network coding in WMN

vi. Routing towards transmission size and computation overhead reduction

HOP COUNT BASED ROUTING PROTOCOLS IN WMN

Routing is a method of sending data packet from source node to receiver node and also the overall communication across the network depends on it. Routing protocols can be generally partitioned into either proactive or reactive depending on how they learn routing path proactively as needed.

Moreover, proactive protocols are much efficient with respect to packet delay and comparatively efficient when number of flow increases.

To increase the throughput, network coding has been incorporated in wireless networks. There are various issues in employing network coding in wireless mesh networks: i.e. to identify packets that are encoded together and to employ the coding conditions in routing protocols.

Akyildiz &Wang (2009) have presented Light Client Management Routing Protocols (LCMR) that proactively selects the routing path from the source to destination, whereas the path between the clients and the routers of the network is in the reactive way. The hop count metric is used to determine the best route. In this protocol, routers service two routing tables: one for local clients of the network and the other for client and remote routers to achieve the routing function of the routers. Based on the information of LCMR protocol stored, the destination routing path is selected. Resources are used significantly based on the instance servicing of two tables.

Avokh & Mirjalily (2013) have described a new load-aware dynamic cost function to weight the links of the network in Multi-Channel Multi-Radio WMNs (MCMR-WMNs). The problem of load balancing and the advantages of Wireless Broadcast Advantage (WBA) were considered in this function. A Load-balanced Multicast Tree Routing (LMTR) algorithm is introduced to provide a balanced multicast trees by making use of the defined cost function. This on-demand routing scheme not only minimizes the number of transmissions, and also reduce the interference and distributed traffic among the nodes in the wireless mesh network. The trade-off between load balancing and network delay can be controlled by this algorithm.

Kandah *et al.* (2012) have focused a DIverse Path ROuting (*DIPRO*) problem, and presented an effective heuristic algorithm for each dynamic request, which seeks a pair of link-disjoint paths, due to any single link failure in the wireless mesh networks. They have also discussed how to provide survivability for dynamic network traffic using multi-path scheme, where user's requests possess random arrival times. Interference and reusability factors are considered when providing multiple paths for each request.

Johnson *et al.* (1996) have proposed a Dynamic Source Routing Algorithm (DSR) which is one of the most commonly used routing protocols in WMNs and it belongs to the group of unicast reactive protocols. To get knowledge of complete routing information to reach its destination for any packet, DSR protocol uses source routing. The performance occurs in the two consecutive stages: the route discovery phase and the route maintenance phase. In the route discovery process, the source node intends to send broadcast packets that include the destination address, the source address and a unique id to neighbouring nodes. Every node, which receives this packet, checks if ithas route information to destination. If not, it adds its own address to route record of the packet and forwards the packet to its neighbours. A route reply is generated, if the route request reaches either the destination itself or an intermediate node which has route information to the destination. In route maintenance phase, updated stored route information is supervised by the nodes using generated Route Error packets (RERR) and it is forwarded towards the source node. By receiving a packet, given router is removed from the database. Thus, a packet that has reached its destination has its header information on the end-to-end connection path. The main drawback of DSR protocol is that it has increased traffic overhead, as it contains complete route information in each of its data packet. This process degrades the routing performance of DSR.

Bhagwat *et al.* (1994) have deployed a Destination Sequence Distance Vector Routing Protocol (DSDV) based on classical Bellman-Ford routing mechanism. All the nodes in the network have a routing table which includes the information of all possible destinations within the network. Sequence numbers are used to differentiate stale routes from fresh ones. To maintain reliability, routing tables are updated periodically throughout the network. If two updates have same sequence numbers, the path with smaller metric is used to optimize the path. DSDV is a proactive unicast routing protocol and it supports bi-directional links.

Perkins *et al.* (1999) proposed Ad-Hoc On-Demand Distance Vector (AODV) Routing protocol that employs simple mechanisms of the type "question - reply" to define routing paths. To achieve this, three types of packets are used: Route Request (RREQ), Route Reply (RREP) and Route Error (RERR). The source node sends RREQ packets to the intermediate to know the route of the destination node. An intermediate node sends an RERR packet when it does not know the route. This process is repeated until the packets reach the destination node. Then, the destination node sends a RREP packet towards the source node. The RREP packet is selected based on the first RREQ reaches the destination from different routes. AODV is an advanced development of DSDV and DSR, as it reduces the number of required broadcasts by creating routes on-demand basis (Pirzada et al 2007).

Kandah *et al.* (2012) have presented a DIverse Path ROuting (*DIPRO*) problem, and present an effective heuristic algorithm for each dynamic request, which seek a pair of link-disjoint paths due to any single link failure in the network. They also discussed about how to provide survivability for dynamic network traffic using multi-path scheme, where users' requests have random arrival times. Interference and reusability factors were considered when providing multiple paths for each request.

Marwaha *et al.* (2009) have initiated a Wireless Mesh Routing (WMR) which uses a reactive route discovery. HELLO messages are used in WMR for topology discovery. The message carries information of the hop count between the sender and the mesh router, and this information in the HELLO packet is called the *distance tag*. Flooding based reactive route discovery is used for the nodes, which are within the mesh group and for outside the mesh group, the restriction of a route discovery is provided. Moreover, using the distance tag information, the mesh router selects the route with minimum number of hops in the route discovery process and the distance tag has to be broadcasted very frequently. This is because new paths can be formed, due to mobility changes in between two HELLO messages. Furthermore, HELLO messages cause considerable control overhead. The route discovery may fail, if the destination node moves to another mesh group. Also, if the destination node moves to the same mesh group, a route discovery for a node outside the mesh group may also fail, since the route discovery would be distance constrained and heading towards the mesh router.

Zoican (2008) has proposed a hybrid routing algorithm called an Intelligent Portal Routing Algorithm (IPRA), for wireless mesh networks. In IPRA, the mesh portal broadcasts a mesh update message periodically and it populates the route towards the mesh portal in the routing table for each of the mesh points. IPRA also allows the use of intelligent mesh portals and mesh points to further improve the performance of mesh network. The packet delivery ratio using IPRA is the same for all 'Network Update' intervals in fixed scenario and it is higher than AODV. This improvement in packet delivery ratio happens due to the partially permanent routing entry of mesh portal in IPRA. Further, in static scenarios, the link breakage frequency is small and therefore, the penalty due to link breakages is small. The routing overhead incurred with IPRA protocol is lower than that of AODV.

Mustapha Boushaba *et al.* (2017) have proposed a unique technique called Node Stability-based Routing (NSR) for selecting the stable nodes on the computing path from source to gateways for the prevention of high levels of network instability which leads to interferences, packet losses and high delays. NSR uses the entropy function to define node stability and a probability function to choose a respective gateway. Through this novel method, frequent rerouting is prevented and fairness is obtained in spreading traffic along the gateways in the network.

OPPORTUNISTIC ROUTING IN WMN

Yuan *et al,* (2005) have proposed Resilient Opportunistic Mesh Routing (ROMER) which balances long-term route stability and perform the short-term opportunistic routing. Set of candidate rules is offered by forwarding mesh on a per packet basis to build a runtime. The forwarding part of the packet opportunistically adapts to the dynamic channel condition to develop the resilience against law ceilings and mesh components failure under DOS attack. ROMER develops redundant data copies in an inhibited and randomised manner over the candidate forwarding mesh. Resilience and performance are enhanced in ROMER compared to single part routing protocol in mesh networks. ROMER proposes path diversity by transmitting to multiple receivers to recover link layer retransmissions and repetitive retransmissions. ROMER enables leveraging path diversity to select highest link opportunistically.

Anonymous Network Coding (ANOC) (Zhang et al 2012) algorithm has applied the idea of cooperative networking. ANOC is built based on the classic Onion Routing protocol and resolves its deviation with network coding by establishing efficient cooperation among relay nodes.

Kurth *et al.* (2008) have presented Transmit Diversity Cooperative Opportunistic Routing (TDiCOR) protocol to improve the over-all throughput performance in Wireless Multi-hop networks. The destructive effects of fading are overcome by the co-operation of neighboring nodes through simultaneous transmission. The robustness of acknowledgements and data transmissions have been increased by distributed transmit diversity using TDiCOR. This algorithm provided opportunistic routing for multiple sources and multiple forwarding nodes in order to optimize the network performance.

Biswas & Morries (2005) have depicted an Extreme Opportunistic Routing (EXOR) protocol that integrates routing and MAC protocol to improve the throughput of large unicast transmissions in multihop wireless networks. It operates on "node's fragment" batch map that constraints batch of packets to reduce the communication cost of agreement. In EXOR, each packet includes a copy of the sender's batch map that has the guess of the highest priority node to receive the packet in the batch. Batches forward the packet from the source to the intermediate nodes. Intermediate nodes themselves choose which one of them will be the node that will forward the packet in the next stage of transmission. The cost of the link based ETX metric is computed to make the decisions. For avoiding duplication, EXOR selects the 'best' receiver of each packet to forward the data. EXOR has improved the performance by enchanting the benefit of long distance but lossy links have would be avoided by traditional Routing protocols.

Rozner *et al.* (2009) have proposed a Simple Opportunistic Adaptive Routing (SOAR) protocol to support multiple simultaneous flows in WMN to avoid duplicate transmission. SOAR uses an adaptive forwarding path selection algorithm to accomplish path diversity while minimizing duplicate retransmission. It constrained the forwarders to be near or along the shortest path based on the ETX route metric. It forwards the packet only from the 'best' forwarding node which is selected by priority timer based forwarders set. It also uses local loss recovery scheme to resourcefully detect and retransmit the lost packets. It utilizes the adaptive rate control scheme for an appropriate sending rate, according to the current network conditions similar to TCP's congestion window. Overhead is reduced by complex acknowledgement scheme and ACK compression techniques. As a result, there is better performance achieved in large range of topologies and in traffic demands.

ROUTING METRICS FOR WIRELESS MESH NETWORKS

Path selection is a process of selecting one path from a list of possibilities route for a packet from the source to its destination. The best route is selected by applying a proper route metrics to multiple routes. Selection of route metrics is an important property which consists any value used by routing algorithms and it determines better performance (Campista et al 2008). A metric includes the information such as bandwidth, network delay, packet loss rate, hop count, node reliability and communication cost. All the metrics serve to represent the link cost between two nodes in the network(Ahmeda et al 2010, Yang & Wang(2008)).

Traditional and most popular link metric in WMNs is HOP count. It computes the path, based on the number of routers transmit the packets from the source node to destination node or number of point-to-point link in the transmission path. The intermediate node in this route metric receives the packet from the source node and modifies the packet by incrementing the hop count by one. It also compares the hop count against a predetermined limit and discards the packet, if the hop count is too high. This avoids packets from endlessly bouncing around the network, due to routing errors. The most conventional routing protocols such as Ad hoc On-Demand Distance Vector (AODV), Dynamic Source Routing (DSR) and Optimized Link State Routing

(OLSR) use hop count to select the best path. When calculating the link cost, this metric does not consider speed, packet loss ratio, reliability, transmission rate and interference.

Cunha *et al.* (2008) have proposed an Expected Transmission Count (ETX) route metric to calculate the expected transmission count in each link along the path from the source to the destination. It broadcasts the probe packet to nearby nodes and also computes the link loss ratio and interlinks interference. Based on the measurements, it estimates the expected number of attempt needed to transmit the packet to the destination successfully. ETX determines the route with the highest probability of distributing the packets rather than one with a shortest path. Compared to hop count, ETX creates more overhead but can be negligible when considering the increase in throughput. If the packets are significantly large, the link performance of the ETX degrades. ETX route metric is helped to ignore the lossy links, high interference links and also asymmetric links. It is independent of the network load to discover high throughput paths in multi-hop wireless links. ETX is isotonic and it is allowed to calculate a minimum weight and loop-free paths. It only captures link loss ratio by ignoring the interference experienced by the links which have a significant impact on the link quality and the data rate at which packets are transmitted over each link. ETX routes the packet through heavily loaded nodes and it leads to unbalanced resource usage.

Schmitz *et al.* (2004) have introduced a Potential Transmission Count (PTC) based on the total number of packets transmission and successful retransmission required in a link to send a packet. PTC is calculated as the inverse of the probability of successful transmission.

Paris *et al.* (2011) have proposed an Expected For Warding counter (EFW) route metric with the combination of ETX and forwarding behaviour.

Nodes in WMNs have a tendency to be selfish in order to improve their network utilization by giving priority to their own traffic and dropping selected packets from neighbouring nodes/routers. To avoid the selfish behaviour of nodes, EFW metric considers the forwarding reliability of relaying nodes in its path calculation to improve the network throughput.

De Couto *et al.* (2003) have computed Expected Transmission Time (ETT) route metric which is an improvement over ETX, as it includes the bandwidth in its computation. The ETT metric estimates the time required to transmit a data packet on a link successfully. In this, the sender node sends two back-to-back probes to its neighbouring nodes and the neighbouring nodes then conclude the Inter-arrival time between the two packets and report to the sender. Sender node computes link capacity from the delay samples. ETT can be calculated by adjusting the ETX metric according to the packet size and the transmission capacity of the link. ETT is suitable for short routes with fewer hops in the network. It is not suitable for longer paths and it could have multiple links that can transmit concurrently because they are not in same contention domain.

Zhong *et al.* (2006) have computed the Expected Anypath Transmission (EAX) route metric that captures the expected number of transmissions from the source node to the destination node and helps to estimate the contribution of a candidate to the delivery of packets between a pair of nodes under opportunistic forwarding. EAX metric selects only those nodes that really help efficient packet delivery by considering both the distance and the link quality. EAX chooses it's forwarding candidates more specifically. It reduces traffic and provides a more reliable transmission in the network.

De couto *et al.* (2003) have presented a Weighted Cumulative Expected Transmission Time (WCETT) similar to ETX. It assigns a weight to each link and that is equal to the expected amount of time that it would take to transmit a packet of some fixed size on that link successfully. It finds the path based on the least sum of ETT and the accounts of intra-flow interference. This expected time depends on the link bandwidth and loss rate. WCETT is an end-to-end route metric because it considers all channels used along the route to avoid intra-flow interference and also provides support for multi-radio or multi-channel wireless networks. This metric is designed to favour channel diverse paths. It suffers to estimate the effective link share and captures interflow interference. The effect of interflow interference is not considered in WCETT, owing to this, it establishes routes which suffer from high levels of interference.

Ali *et al.* (2014) have proposed a Dynamic Weighted Cumulative Expected Transmission Time (D-WCETT) route metric which is an advanced version of the WCETT. This route metrics form routes based on the network load information. This routing metric chooses the paths dynamically with least level of congestion by considering locally available queue information.

Wang *et al.* (2005a) have presented a Load Aware Expected Transmission Time (LAETT) route metric to incorporate the load balancing and link quality component in ETT. Load aware ETT is a combination of Expected Transmission Time for a node to transmit the packet successfully and Remaining Capacity (RC) on the node. RC of link is used as load aware parameter to balance the traffic on the network. If two paths have same value of ETX, then LAETT will prefer the paths with high value of RC. Loop free route or isotonic nature of the LAETT calculates the weights on each link. It captures link quality and traffic load without considering intra flow and inter flow interferences.

Draves *et al.* (2004) have proposed a Modified Expected Number of Transmissions (mETX) as an improvement over ETX to calculate the bit error probability using the location of the corrupted bit in the probe and the corresponding bit error all over the consecutive transmission. This route metric is able to estimate the path which has minimal interferences, higher-throughput and nominal transmission time. It is observed that ETX does not take the channel variability into account and only considers the average channel behaviour but mETX considers critical channel variability at the time of packet transmission.

Wang *et al.* (2005 b) have presented a Metric of Interference and Channel Switching (MIC) route metric which considers interflow interference and intra-flow interference. The MIC metric overcomes the limitations of WCETT by solving its problems of inability to capture inter-flow interference. In this route metric, each node calculates the interflow interference by counting the number of interfering nodes in the neighbourhood and utilizes the measurements of signal power in the multihop networks. In MIC, Overhead occurs to maintain and update information of the ETT for each link and it can significantly affect the network performance depending on traffic loads. It captures intra-flow interference only in two consecutive links.

Yifei *et al.* (2009) have introduced an Interference avoidance and Coding aware Metric (ICM) which investigates a tradeoff between performance gain and degradation of functionality, due to the interference in multiple unicast sessions. ICM metric combines the interference cost and coding gain to compute the best path. Simulation results show that ICM based routing protocols have enhanced the functional performance of network throughput and reduced the end -to-end delay in the wireless mesh networks.

Subramanian *et al.* (2006) have described an Interference Aware Routing Metric (iAWARE) for Multi-Radio Mesh Networks. iAWARE captures the effects of variation in link loss-ratio and transmission rate as well as interflow and intra-flow interferences. This metric concentrates on the aforementioned limitations of existing metrics such as hop count, ETX, ETT, WCETT, MIC in Wireless mesh networks. This routing metric finds paths with less congestion, low level of interference, low packet drop ratio and high data rate. This will result in the iAWARE metric choosing a path with lower ETT but higher interference. iAWARE maintains many of the properties of WCETT with the exemption of its handling of inter-flow interference measurements. It directly measures the average interference generated by neighbouring nodes.

ROUTING TOWARDS THROUGHPUT AND END -TO-END DELAY IMPROVEMENT

Kudret *et al.* (2018) have proposed Power Allocation and Routing for Full-duplex Multi Hop Wireless Networks under Full Interference. Despite routing process, a power allocation solution has been developed for allowing full duplex in the multi hop wireless networks under full interference. First, for enhancing end-to-end throughput of full duplex transferring on known path, an optimization problem is formulated under the consideration of full interference model. In order to provide the best transmit power, a linear programming based solution has been devised for FD passing nodes on the path. Then, Dijkstra's algorithm has been modified by employing the given power allocation for the computation of path metrics.

Jilong Li *et al.* (2018) have proposed a clustering based routing algorithm taking into consideration of an interference and load balancing routing metric that emphasizes on reducing the issues of existing networks. Also, a scheme has been developed and it considers both the qualities on the whole route to destination for reducing the end-to-end delay. In addition, mesh station channel interference and queue information are utilized appropriately to overcome the notified challenges.

Jing Chen *et al.* (2016) have developed a Distributed Greedy Coding-aware Deterministic Routing (DGCDR) for multi-flow coding in wireless networks. So as to increase coding opportunities, a decoding policy and a coding condition are constructed in the multi-flow environment and they use the coding advantage of multiple intersecting flows in a greedy manner. There by, it achieves increased coding benefit, high throughput, smaller queue size and decreased delay.

Minho Jeong *et al.* (2016) have proposed a distributed coding aware routing protocol through which throughput is maximized and delay of real-time multimedia flows is minimized in wireless multi hop networks. This scheme works based on dynamic source routing mechanism which finds the route considering the network coding opportunities along with traffic load balancing capability. Furthermore, the network coding overhead is reduced at intermediate nodes by selecting a route with only single possibility of network coding. They have shown that this new mechanism outperforms the DCAR with respect to throughput and delay.

Koksal & Balakrishnan (2006) have proposed a *Quality-aware* routing protocol. The choice of the routing path with the smallest number of hop-count between two nodes frequently leads to poor performance, since those routing paths have a tendency to use links that could have marginal quality. Thus, *quality-aware* routing metrics are preferred for networks that are built exclusively from wireless radios. These metrics are proposed to maximize the network performance and also to diminish the loss rates visible to higher layer protocols like TCP. Two new metrics such as modified expected number of transmissions (mETX) and effective number of transmissions (ENT) are explained and they work well under an ample diversity of channel conditions.

Laufer *et al.* (2009) have described a novel routing paradigm called Shortest Multi-rate Anypath First routing (SMAF) which take a broad view of opportunistic routing in WMN. SMAF algorithm presents a solution to integrate opportunistic routing and multiple transmission rates for best possible route selection. To minimize the distance to the destination, SMAF algorithm find a forwarding set and a transmission rate for each node optimally. This rate is used to broadcast a packet to the nodes in the set and among them one node forwards the packet to the destination. To solve the rate finding and forwarding set to a given destination, Expected anypath transmission time (EATT) route metric is used. They presented that multi-rate any path routing performs better than any path routing.

Marwaha *et al.* (2009) have presented a Wireless Mesh Routing (WMR) which uses a reactive route discovery. The HELLOW message carries the information of the hop count between the sender and the mesh router, and this information in the HELLO packet is called the *distance tag whichprovides the topology discovery*. Flooding based reactive route discovery is used for the nodes. It will be placed within the mesh group and outside the mesh group and the limitation of route discovery to the mesh groups is provided. Furthermore, using the distance tag information, the mesh router decides the route with minimum number of hops in the route discovery process and the distance tag has to be broadcasted very frequently. Because of that, new routing paths can be formed, due to mobility changes in between two HELLO messages. Furthermore, HELLO messages cause considerable control overhead. The route discovery may fail, if the destination node moves to another mesh group. Also, if the destination node moves to the same mesh group, a route discovery for a node outside the mesh group may also fail, while the route discovery process based on distance constrained is heading towards the mesh router.

Zoican (2008) introduced an Intelligent Portal Routing Algorithm (IPRA) which is a hybrid routing algorithm for wireless mesh networks. In IPRA, a mesh updates message broadcasts by the mesh portal periodically and it populates the route towards the mesh portal for each of the mesh points in the routing table. By using intelligent mesh portals and mesh points, IPRA algorithm improves the performance of mesh network. The packet delivery ratio using IPRA is the same for all intervals of "Network Update" in fixed scenario and it is higher than the AODV. This enhancement in packet delivery ratio is due to the partially permanent routing entry of mesh portal in IPRA. The link breakage frequency is small in static scenarios and because of that, the penalty due to link breakages is small. The IPRA protocol has minimal routing overhead compared to AODV Routing Protocol.

Roy *et al.* (2008) have proposed low-overhead adaptive online algorithm called ODMRP and also described the routing metrics for high-throughput tree or mesh structure in multicast protocols. They have pointed up the important difference between unicast and multicast routing and also provided the details of transmission of data packets in the link layer. ODMRP algorithm is used to incorporate link-quality metrics to a multicast routing protocol. Simulation results show that ODMRP equipped with any of the link-quality-based routing metrics is able to achieve higher throughput than the other routing algorithms.

Liu & Liao (2006) have described an efficient approach to improve the network capacity and to utilize multiple channels in wireless multi-hop networks. Based on the assumptions that the nodes are stationary and each of them is equipped with one or more NICs. A new proposed, Bottleneck Link Capacity (BLC) path metric is used to select the path which has the maximum residual capacity. An on-demand routing protocol called Capacity-Aware Routing (CAR) is developed based on the BLC route metric. This BLC route metric shows the enhanced performance compared to hop count metrics and Weighted Cumulative ETT (WCETT) in terms of system throughput and end-to-end packet delay and the proposed routing mechanism is a scalable solution for multi-channel wireless mesh networks.

Siddiqui *et al.* (2007) have proposed a secured multi-path hybrid routing protocol to improve the reliability of wireless mesh networks. It uses proactive as well as reactive routing methods to find the routes from source to the destination. When a route is lost, this algorithm finds alternative routes and also provides a secure reliable routing. Efficient techniques of MHRP have better throughput with less latency and control overhead by consuming minimum amount of energy at each node.

ROUTING TOWARDS TRANSMISIION SIZE AND COST REDUCTION

Ashish Nanda *et al.* (2018) have presented a secure Geo-Location Oriented Routing (SecureGLOR) protocol for wireless mesh networks in which hybrid encryption scheme is employed for its multilevel security framework. Here, the network's overall performance has been increased compared to the basic encryption by a combination of symmetric key along with the asymmetric key encryption. Transmitted data size and computation over-head have been reduced and faster encryption-decryption cycles have been obtained.

Yaping Liang *et al.* (2017) have proved that the length of the data packets also will affect the network coding performance and energy consumption. Using this fact, they have proposed a new strategy of network coding using packet length in order to improve the coding gain. In this method, the smaller packets are bundled with the large one in the same waiting queue to enhance the coding gain in the asynchronous network coding and the old packets are replaced with the larger one. Then it is coded with the other waiting queue there by effect of packet length will get reduced.

Phong *et al.* (2016) have suggested an instantaneous recovery route design with multiple coding-aware link protection in order to obtain higher link cost reduction in the network. Here, two novel scenarios are included namely traffic splitting and two sources and a unique destination which have been used to combine multiple sources and destination. They have proposed two phrases involving identification of route path for all possible sources and destinations with the intention of reducing total cost. Network coding has been employed in the common path of the second phases. The performance of this scheme increases proportionally to the average node degree in the network.

ShaobinCai *et al.* (2015) have presented a Multiple Path and Network Coding transport protocol for under water acoustic sensor network in which two groups of packets (A,B) are coded after having established three unique paths that are transmitted over two side paths correspondingly. Again another two group of packets C=AEBB are transmitted through the middle path. So as to avoid the number of duplicate packets without losing the transmission reliability, group C packets are coded again by network coding based on the link error and reliable transport protocol i.e. Twin Path and Network Coding. Similar data delivery ratio with lower energy consumption can be acquired for TPNC compared to MPNC.

Cunbo Lu *et al.* (2015) have presented a low-jitter wireless transmission algorithm based on buffer management (BLJCAR) in which packets are decided in the coding node based on the queue length based threshold policy rather than the regular opportunistic network coding used in the existing coding aware routing. This method is referred as a unified framework to merge the single rate with the multiple rate case. BLJCAR has two phases i.e. network jitter training and data transmission and in the data transmission phase, packets are chosen in coding node based on the queue-length based threshold policy. Jitter training phase is employed to identify the optimal threshold of the queue-length control policy. With respect to jitter, packet delivery delay, packet loss ratio and network throughput in network congestion, this method outperforms the traditional coding aware routing algorithms.

Lei Wang *et al.* (2012) have done the research on energy efficiency of wireless sensor networks with Network Coding-based Multipath Routing (NCMR) which is based on linear network coding. Braided multipath network is utilized for encoding packets at source nodes. As network coding is done with multipath routing, number of routes and transmission time are reduced in sensor network and they lead to energy consumption of NCMR as well as reliability.

Yan Yan *et al.* (2010) have combined the opportunistic routing and the network coding (CORE) for enhancing the performance of a WMN by proposing coding-aware opportunistic routing mechanism through which CORE is able to fully utilize the broadcast properties of a wireless channel and tolerate packet loss. The next hop node is allowed with the most coding gain for the continuation of packet forwarding and also it tries to make best use of the number of packets that are passed in a single transmission. Through this method, numbers of transmissions are reduced considerably. COPE is not the best choice in the lossy wireless environments, since in such an environment, the FIFO strategy will lead to penalty on coding opportunities which are bounded by the number of neighbors that have overheard some of these queue head packets. Hence, the performance of COPE is suboptimal in lossy environments.

Jing Chen *et al.* (2015) have suggested a Connected Dominating Set (CDS)-based Flow-oriented Coding-aware Routing (CFCR) technique to improve potential coding opportunities. Upon overcoming coding collision problem of flows by incorporating information confirmation process, it leads to decrease in the failure rate of coding. In addition, the proposed routing process takes the advantage of CDs and flow coding, respectively. Through this proposed coding, reliable transmission, higher throughput and reduced cost can be obtained.

NETWORK CODING IN WMN

Network Coding (NC) allows the intermediate Forwarding Nodes (FNs) to encode and then forward the data packets to enhance the efficiency of multicast content distribution over multi-hop wireless networks.

Katti *et al.* (2006) have proposed a practical network coding based, packet forwarding architecture (COPE) routing algorithm that improves the throughput of wireless mesh networks. COPE incorporates three main techniques: opportunistic listening, opportunistic coding and learning neighbour state to reduce the number of necessary transmission. Initially, the practical network coding system COPE improves the performance of multi hop wireless network compared to the traditional routing. Here, the packet can be decoded completely by every next hop of encoded packets. This coding opportunity limits the COPE with in two hop regions and it can't detect a route with more coding opportunists.

Han *et al.* (2008) have presented a Coding-Aware Multi-Path routing protocol (CAMP), that forwards the packets over multiple paths dynamically based on the path reliability and coding opportunity. CAMP proposes a new route discovery and forwarding mechanism based on the ETX route metric that splits the traffic among multiple paths and actively creates coding opportunity by switching its path to maximize the switching gain.

Sadaf Talha *et al.* (2017) have utilized network coding for wireless body area network for the consumption of energy transmission. Here, the sensor nodes deployed in the patient's body for the monitoring of diseases come down quickly by the limited battery power. But, the sensor nodes need to collect the data and send it to the sink node continuously. Thus, it requires energy efficient communication methods. Through network coding, spectrum and energy efficient technique will be utilized to transmit several user data streams in single end-to-end cooperative transmission in wireless body area networks. Experimental results show improved bit error rate for the first user apart from the second user data. Getting two copies of the same data from the diverse paths gives enhancement for combining techniques.

Jing Chen *et al.* (2016) have developed a Distributed Greedy Coding-aware Deterministic Routing (DGCDR) protocol for multi flow wireless environment for enhancing the potential coding opportunities with decoding policy. As multi-flow coding can improve the coding benefit in complex network, a greedy aggregation method and greedy coding algorithm are also proposed to sense and avoid the multi flow interference at the time of route discovery. Link quality and path length route metric are considered to evaluate a specific route, particularly for multiple candidate routes between source and destination node. In addition to the design of confirmation process in the protocol increased coding benefit, decreased delay, larger throughput, and smaller queue size are obtained.

Long Hai *et al.* (2014) have proposed a novel High-throughput Coding-aware Opportunistic Routing (HCOR) to obtain the maximal throughput gain in wireless mesh networks. HCOR emphasises on anypath routing and makes use of the network coding gain to identify the route with minimal anypath cost rationally. In addition, this method acts as multihop network coding and keeps changing the route with dynamical data loads. Through these novel methods, it is confirmed that HCOR outperforms well in terms of high throughput than the coding opportunity-aware routing.

Rami Halloush *et al.* (2016) have suggested a novel reliable multicast protocol called HopCaster that uses network coding with hop-by-hop transport. In HopCaster, there will be no requirement for computing the number of coded packets for the transmission through forwarding node in order to avoid packet retransmissions. HopCaster also addresses the issues of heterogeneous multicast receivers. Furthermore, a cross-layer multicast rate adaptation mechanism is developed which makes HopCaster to enhance multicast throughput by modifying wireless transmission rate dynamically based on the changes in receiver populations and channel conditions.

Xie *et al.* (2013) have done survey on inter-flow network coding (XNC), which is termed to be a form of network coding and it takes encoding of various flows for the benefit of wireless mesh networks with either reliable or lossy links. Here, they have presented a survey on XNC in WMNs for unicast traffic, with multiple design factors regarding XNC. Two types of WMNs have been considered i.e. one with reliable links and the other with lossy links. The survey depicts clearly of how XNC can be utilized successfully in both the types of WMNs.

Gin-Xian Kok *et al.* (2015) have proposed Network Coding RouTing (NCRT) protocol which considers both coding opportunities and network workload. NCRT is the modification of the Dynamic Source Routing (DSR) protocol developed by Johnson *et al.* (2001) and a new set of coding conditions has been developed and called as Improved Generalized Coding Conditions (IGCC) to obtain more coding opportunities. It utilizes coding-aware and load-aware routing measures so as to make use of the network coding benefit.

As present routing schemes using network coding either passively wait for potential coding opportunities or fail to reflect the spirit of wireless interference, researchers intent to alleviate the critical issues such as limited frequency resources, interference, noise and channel fading for improving the throughput of WMNs, Yuhuai Peng *et al.* (2013) have developed novel Coding and Interference Aware Routing (CIAR) which detects potential coding opportunities actively in establishing paths but also considers the interference cost while path selection. The CIAR protocol is used to make the tradeoffs in routing choices among facilitating more coding gains and mitigating interference. The results demonstrate that the CIAR protocol performs better than other schemes with respect to buffer overflow probability, average end-to-end throughput and average end-to-end delay.

Scheuermann *et al.* (2007) have proposed a novel routing protocol Near-Optimal Coordinated Coding (noCoCo) which is an extension to COPE and is able to generate and maximize coding opportunities in a more deterministic way between opposite directional flows. This cross-layer approach for bidirectional flows is used to integrate per-hop scheduling, Network coding and congestion control. No CoCo shows enhanced performance compared to COPE in terms of delay, transmission overhead and network throughput.

Chaporkar & Proutiere (2007) have presented an advancement of COPE known as XOR-Sym routing algorithm to encode the packets using XOR operation for symmetric flows (where the source of one routing flow is the destination of the other flow without requirement of opportunistic listening). XOR-Sym algorithm decodes the packets, only at their destinations and not at intermediate relays. Intermediate nodes do not perform any decoding function and only liable to perform the XOR operation for encoding the data packets. Storage of recently transmitted packets (at the source node of a flow) and XOR operations only between two specific flows are the limitations of XOR-Sym algorithm. The implementation complexity of XOR-Sym network coding scheme is lesser than COPE but both have similar benefits.

Rozner *et al.* (2007) have implemented an Efficient Retransmission (ER) routing protocol for wireless LANs. Based on the concept of modified COPE, this algorithm has improved the efficiency of MAC layer retransmission for the lost packets, in unicast and multicast traffic of wireless networks. ER has proposed a light-weight receiver feedback scheme and scheduling algorithm to determine which packets need to be retransmitted and also proposed a coding algorithm to optimize which set of packets to be coded together. In this, lost packets from different destinations are encoded instead of retransmitting the lost packets in original form. So that, coding based retransmissions efficiently reduce the number of retransmissions required to recover packet losses and increase the performance gain in multicast traffic.

Rozner *et al.* (2007) have implemented an Efficient Retransmission (ER) routing protocol for wireless LANs. Based on the concept of modified COPE, this algorithm has improved the efficiency of MAC layer retransmission for the lost packets, in unicast and multicast traffic of wireless networks. ER has proposed a light-weight receiver feedback scheme and scheduling algorithm to determine which packets need to be retransmitted and also proposed a coding algorithm to optimize which set of packets to be coded together. In this, lost packets from different destinations are encoded instead of retransmitting the lost packets in original form. So that, coding based retransmissions efficiently reduce the number of retransmissions required to recover packet losses and increase the performance gain in multicast traffic.

Centralized Network Coding Aware Routing

Ni *et al.* (2006) have proposed routing with opportunistically coded Exchange (ROCX) to reduce the total number of coded transmissions. Expected number of Coded Transmission (ECX) route metric is used to estimate the successful exchange of encoded packets between pair of nodes through a coding point. ROCX is an optimal coding aware routing mechanism used to compute the average number of transmissions per flow using ECX route metric. ROCX routing protocol reduces the number of transmissions compared to COPE and shows the better performance for long distance flows and high data rates.

Sengupta *et al.* (2007) have proposed a Linear Programming based Formulation (LPF) routing algorithms consisting of several coding aware inter-flows, that quantify the impact of joint network coding and interference aware routing schemes. LPF algorithms have two components i) 'close to each other' which is used for utilizing coding opportunities and ii) 'away from each other' which is used to avoid wireless interference. Based on the awareness of network coding opportunity, LPF algorithms compute source-destination routes and enhance coding opportunities to maximize the network throughput of unicast traffic in any wireless network topology. Their simulation shows that, the selection of routes using network coding leads to a higher end-to-end throughput compared to the coding oblivious routing algorithms.

Rayanchu *et al.* (2008) have proposed a network Coding with LOss awareNEss (CLONE) to concentrate on an adequate redundancy in local network coding operations in unicast flows under lossy wireless environments thereby achieving further performance gains in multi-hop wireless scenarios. First, the practical network coding structure COPE does not provide protection against losses on the wireless path directly, but loss-aware CLONE clearly uses redundancy in the design of network coding structures to guard against the negative impacts of such losses. CLONE algorithm uses a relay node which optimizes a coding strategy, explicitly sends out information to packet header through the possible decoding paths for each packet, thus making the trivial decoding strategy. CLONE schemes realize low post coding loss rates and this enhancement depends on a number factor such as the flow structure, overhearing pattern of the nodes, degree of the nodes and the link loss rates.

Distributed Network Coding Aware Routing

More numbers of distributed coding-aware routing techniques have been proposed to overcome the limitations of centralized coding aware routing. Distributed coding-aware routing approaches are able to detect coding opportunities on the entire path from the source to the destination and improve the network throughput. Each node in the distributed coding-aware routing is responsible for creating a local routing decision based on the previous maintained network state information.

Wei *et al.* (2009) have presented a Network Coding Aware Routing Protocol (NCAR) for lossy wireless network. The problem of finding the best coding solution at intermediate nodes, when there exists more than one unicast flow and more than one coding scheme, is solved by NCAR Protocol. Potential coding availability in the route discovery process and the link delivery ratio in the best possible route selection are the main concerns of NCAR. Coding condition with priority determination, route discovery process, and route selection process are the important considerations of NCAR routing algorithm.

The main function of 'Coding conditions with a priority determination' is to find more than one coding opportunity scheme which combines the different unicast flows at intermediate nodes during the path discovery process. Based on the Ad hoc On-Demand Distance Vector, RREQ (Route REQuest) and RREP (Route REPly) mechanism. NCAR route discovery process determines the priorities for the existing coding schemes in the network. Based on the consideration of link delivery ratio and coding opportunities of each node, NCAR selects the optimal path in the 'route selection processes'. NCAR uses an improved ECX metric which is responsible for reducing the Expected Transmission Count based on the Network Coding (ETC-NC) value for different coding schemes. NCAR outperforms than the network performances of COPE and traditional routing.

Zhou *et al.* (2010) have presented a Network Joint Coding Aware Routing (NJCAR) which has the ability to find entire potential routes from the sender node to the receiver node and finds multiple hop decoding techniques effectively. With the awareness of maximum coding opportunities, NJCAR algorithm intelligently selects the optimal path for each flow from the sender to the receiver. It achieves the joint decoding by completely utilizing the global state information because of that, it reduces the transmission overhead and increases the possible transmission opportunities. Limitations of decoding structure with in one hop are overcome by NJCAR using changed decoding probability and joint decoding opportunities. Simulation results show that NJCAR outperforms than COPE and improves the network throughput compared to COPE.

Yan *et al.* (2008) have proposed a Rate Adaptive Coding aware Routing (RCR) mechanism to improve the network throughput in wireless networks. Coding aware multipath routing with traffic splitting can increase the coding gain. RCR mechanism uses three metrics i.e Required Transmission

Number (RTN), Matched Coding Rate (MCR) and Congestion Avoidance Rate (CAR) to improve the coding opportunistic. RTN metric specifies the number of required transmission for intermediate nodes to forward a data packet in a particular flow. Information and required amount of traffic for a particular flow, which are coded efficiently with other flows along a path, are provided by MCR route metric. MCR route metric is calculated based on the bottleneck node along a path for that specified flow. The maximal rate of flow allocated for a node without causing congestion is indicated by a CAR routing metric. This routing algorithm has two components i) Route Discovery and ii) Route Maintenance. With the use of On-Demand routing Strategy similar to DSR, RCR algorithms find the multiple paths from source to destination based onthe route metrics using RREQ and RREP cycles. When receiving all RREP's, source node transmits data traffic to the minimal rate allocated to each path. Data packet is received by a destination node and also it checks and updates the required transmission cost along the path.

OCR kai *et al.* (2009) has described an On-demand COPE-aware Routing (OCR) Protocol to enhance the throughput of wireless mesh networks. Compared to COPE, OCR Protocol actively detects coding opportunities in three phases i.e. code judgment, route discovery and route maintenance. Redundant points, which are not suitable for coding application, are eliminated by triple structure label nodes that have the parameters of current node, number of input links to current node and number of output links to the current node. Higher number of input links node is selected as a coding node rather than output links. OCR protocol has the details of status of a packet in the sending queue of a node and the best route is selected from the source to destination in terms of high coding opportunity and lowest hop count. Based on the AODV's route maintenance method, OCR route maintenance phase regularly broadcasts the HELLO packets. Simulation results shows that OCT protocol hasimproved the throughput and transmission rates of WN are compared to traditional AODV with COPE.

OCAR Sun *et al.* (2010) have presented an On demand Coding Aware Routing (OCAR) algorithm which detects the path with more coding opportunities and less interference to achieve higher throughput in wireless mesh networks. OCAR detects the coding opportunities along the entire path from source to destination based on the information of coding aware and interference avoidance route metric. This route metric in path discovery not only incorporates the potential coding opportunity and also considers the effect of variation in link loss ratio, differences in transmission rate and inter and intra flow interferences. OCAR routing algorithm effectively increases the network throughput, reduces end - to - end delay and network congestion and also increases the overall protocol overhead with extra length of control packets excessive PREQ flooding and high storage at intermediate nodes.

Each node in the network maintains the limited state information and also has the response to take route decision which is enabled in hop-by-hop routing. Because of that complexity, protocol overhead is reduced in that routing technique. Wu *et al.* (2007) have implemented a new Markovian Routing Metric(MMR) algorithm for multiple unicast flow in wireless networks. MMR routing metric differs from conventional routing metric where as MMR model calculates the cost of the routing path as a sum of conditional cost on the links but earlier models consider sum of the cost on the individual links. MMR metric is capable of discovering the coding opportunities path and this capability is limited to only knowing the existence of coding opportunity. Hence, it reduces the channel resource consumption. The cost of transmitting a packet across a link depends on the previous link of the packet without considering the knowledge of number of coding opportunities that exist on the link. Markovian Metric Routing integrates with Expected Resource

Consumption (ERC) link metric to improve the system efficiency by maximizing the total resource consumption of a path. Simulation results show have remarkable resource saving and throughput gain.

Yan *et al.* (2008) have proposed a Coding Aware Opportunistic Routing (COAR) to integrate the performance of opportunistic routing and network coding in wireless mesh networks. Based on the utilization of local state information of a node, COAR makes a decision of forwarding a packet, without any synchronization among nodes. COAR algorithm works on three constraints, i.e forwarder set selection, best forwarder selection and priority based forwarding. In forwarder set selection step, each node selects its forwarder set based on direct neighboring node of a sender and distance towards its destination is calculated by ETX. Then, the best forwarder selection selects the higher coding opportunities node as a forwarder for transmitting packets. At the third step i.e. timer based priority forwarding, reduces the synchronization requirements and prevents redundant transmission. COAR considers the impact of variable flow number and path length and improves the throughput of unicast flows in WMNs.

Le *et al.* (2010) have presented a Distributed Coding Aware Routing (DCAR) protocol that has the ability to discover available paths and concurrently find more coding opportunities of the entire paths. DCAR proposes a coding aware routing metric (CRM) that evaluates the performance of a path which may be the coding possible path or coding impossible path. This metric concludes the existing traffic load information for making the evaluation because, the saving in the 'free-ride' bandwidth depends on the existing traffic and also it provides the interpretation of 'free-ride' benefit for coding possible paths transferable to the performance measure of coding impossible paths.

The Multi-Rate Algorithm (MRA) proposed by Vieira *et al.* (2013) transmits the packets without considering the path conditions and capacity such as contention, interference and bandwidth etc. Multi path routing Throughput (MRT) is a novel approach that exploits the attainable bandwidth of the transmitting paths in the presence of neighboring interferences and link error. This has been proposed by Qureshi *et al.* 2014.

Guo *et al.* (2010) have described the Backbone ROuting with Network Coding (BRONC) algorithm for multihop wireless networks. In BRONC, throughput improvement highly depends on the traffic pattern and network topology and also maximum coding gain is achieved, when the pairs of overlapping flows forward in the network. Using the details of pre-specified routes in backbone routing, BRONC increases the possibility of encoding packets at intermediate nodes. Bidirectional nature of flows over the backbone improves the coding opportunities. Transmission overheads and computational complexity for coding decisions within wireless networks are decreased by using BRONC algorithm. The main constraints of BRONC scheme are of: i) no need of opportunistic listening ii) communication overhead is reduced due to local information of the hop view. Simulation results show that BRONC algorithm has the performance improvement fcompared to other coding approaches.

The Coding-aware Opportunistic Routing Algorithm in WMNs (CORMEN) is based on the performance of opportunistic routing and network coding(Islam & Pramod , 2010). Based on the consideration of minimum delay, CORMEN algorithm has the capability to find a coding aware path from the source to the destination. In CORMEN, coordination among the nodes is not required because each node takes the decisions of coding individually. The important features of CORMEN are forwarding node selection, shortest path selection, packet encoding, forwarding time setting and good quality links of forwarding node. Forwarder nodes are selected based on the ETX route metric, threshold limit of ETX between source and destination node and they ensure the good quality links. Shortest path calculated using ETX metric, that constraints the actual path, should be close to the shortest path to avoid paths diverging and duplicate transmissions. Setting forwarding timer of each node depends on the possible coding opportunities, the order of the forwarder set and ETX value of best route from sender to receiver node. Before expiry value of timer, the selected node encodes all possible packets and forwards through the path. Simulation results show that, CORMEN algorithm has the highest throughput and lower end-to-end delay compared to the COPE routing algorithm.

Jiao *et al.* (2008) have presented an Active Network Coding High-throughput Optimizing Routing protocol (ANCHOR) technique for wireless Adhoc networks. It adjusts the routing in the transmission of data packet instead of its path discovery process. The ANCHOR algorithm constraints four components: opportunistic listening, active optimizing routing, Network coding and opportunistic routing. By broadcasting nature of HELLOW messages periodically, nodes are set in promiscuous mode and they interchange the reception reports. During the active optimizing routing phase, a node receives the original data packet and optimizes the route to create a NC opportunity with over-heard packets received already. Encoding of the packets based on the timer value is processed in NC step. The timer starts, when it receives a data packet and it expires when coding of packets are received from reception reports. Nodes in the path analyze the possibility of opportunistic forwarding i.e. verify the ability of node to cancel any further forwarding of a data packet, if a downstream node on the path has received the same packet. In this condition, duty of forwarding data packets towards the destination is performed by downstream node. Implementation and simulation results show that ANCHOR performs better than COPE and DSR in several scenarios.

Comparison of some surveyed non-NC and NC-aware Routing Protocols (RPs) for wireless networks is listed in Table 2.1.

Table 2.1 (Continued)

BRONC	ETX	Backbone enhances network efficiency and capacity. No additional computational cost and communication overhead	BR-NO-Cj RROOCk RR-NO-Cl
CORMEN	ETX	Tight synchronization is not required among nodes	COPE
CORE	Coding-chance-based Metric	High coding gain nodes forward data packets	COPE, CORE without NC
ANCHOR	ETX	Actively optimizes routing to exploit NC potential	COPE DSR
CAMP	ETX	Packet forwarding based on coding opportunities along multipaths	COPE TRP Multipath routing
SMAF	EATT	Best possible route selection	Any path routing
HOR	Anypath routing	Select the route with minimal cost	Non-NC
CIAR	MIC	Considers the interference cost while path selection	Non-NC
QAR	mETX	Works well under an ample diversity of channel conditions	Higher layer protocols like TCP

MOTIVATION OF STUDY

From the above literature review, it has been observed that some tasks have to be achieved in this research work:

- To identify the suitable route metric for wireless mesh networks in order to improve the performance.
- To identify a suitable path selection algorithm using network coding for wireless mesh network.
- To identify an appropriate Opportunistic coding aware routing algorithm for wireless mesh network for the transmission of encoded packets to improve the throughput and also to reduce the delay.
- To identify suitable code-aware and load-aware route metrics that consider both the coding-opportunities and network workload.

OBJECTIVES OF THE STUDY

In the literature review, the existing routing metrics, existing routing protocols, Network coding, Coding opportunistic, their methods and issues regarding the performance of the routing algorithms have been analyzed and through which the following frameworks are attempted to identify suitable essential solutions to attain the best results. The objectives of the dissertation are:

- To develop an Optimal Encoder Selection (OES) algorithm based on the selected route metric to select the optimized encode node among all the possible encoding nodes in the routing path.

- To design an Opportunity Encoder Based Delay Aware Routing (OEDAR) algorithm for wireless mesh network.
- To propose an Adaptive Coding Aware Routing algorithm (ACAR) to encode the packets in two different flows which will not have the intermediate nodes in wireless mesh networks based on the delay and bandwidth constrained anypath cost route metrics.
- To develop a high throughput Network Coding Aware Routing (Net-CART) protocol for wireless mesh networks using Code-aware and Load -aware route metric.

CHAPTER 3

OPPORTUNITY ENCODER BASED DELAY AWARE ROUTING ALGORITHM IN WIRELESS MESH NETWORK

This chapter emphasizes an Opportunity Encoder based Delay Aware Routing algorithm (OEDAR) for enhancing the throughput and reducing the delay using network coding in wireless mesh networks. The main purpose of this algorithm is to resolve whether the network coding must be performed or not and also it decides about which node should be used as the coding node among all the intersecting nodes to obtain the highest throughput gain.

OVERVIEW

The aforementioned empirical survey has paved us a way to formulate a new method which selects an intermediate nodes within two-hop region from the first encoding node rather than first intersecting node which to be considered as encoding node. The major intention of this thesis is to contribute a valuable new method which makes both delay and any path cost when deciding encoding node in the opportunistic routing. The major role of this manuscript is given below.

1. To the best of the researcher's knowledge, to prove that necessary encoding node would be decided by considering all the intersecting nodes for the encoding of packets.

2. Two solutions have been made to design the coding aware Opportunistic Routing (OR) out of these, the first one is the decision in which nodes should be included in the forwarding list for sending the encoded packet and the second one shows how to measure the cost and delay of network in an OR.

3. A novel Optimal Encoder Selection algorithm (OES) which has been proposed, utilizes any path routing for finding out the minimal any path cost and delay of the encoding node in the selector list using network coding. Compared to other existing schemes, OEDAR is believed to be more feasible on selecting coding opportunities. Since OEDAR has been designed on a multi hop network coding structure, huge coding opportunities can also be obtained than the local coding structure (Le *et al.* 2010).

The contribution of this work is to describe an intelligent path selection, based on the quality of the encoded node in wireless mesh networks using network coding and to evaluate its performance by means that of extensive simulations. The main objective of this method is to acquire ample coding benefits as possible in routing for two flow wireless networks and also to increase the throughput as well as reduce the delay using Optimal Encoder Selector (OES) algorithm.

GENERAL CODING CONDITIONS

OEDAR is a coding-aware opportunistic routing method. It generally works between Internet Protocol (IP) and Media Access Control (MAC) layers and a coding layer is inserted to do the computation of delay and cost of forwarding list of encoded node there by serving sending and receiving of encoded packets. OEDAR utilizes XOR based coding method and the basics of

OEDAR are distributed system which uses any path routing. OEDAR algorithm is intended to resolve whether the network coding is supposed to be done and which nodes ought to be used as the encoding nodes to obtain the highest throughput gain. To realize OEDAR, every encoded node within two hop regions will get selected and also each encoded node performs the computation of temporary anypath cost and processing. Further, transmission delay has also been computed independently for each encoded flow. All flows constantly choose the *lowest anypath cost path and minimal delay as* their transmission routes. The central idea is to ensure that every encoded packet should be decoded by the respective receiver. Before exploring into details, the terms used in this work are defined in Table 3.1.

Table 3.1 Terms used in OEDAR

Terms	Definitions
Encoded Packet	An XOR of multiple native (raw) packets
Forwarding list	Set of all new nodes for an intersect node on a flow for packet transmission
Coding node	A node that encodes raw packets together
Decoding node	A node which decodes the encoded packets
Back warding list	Set of all existing nodes for an intersect node on a flow for packet transmission
Virtual flow list	Record of information about the flow and node
Coding structure	Set of nodes and flows for opportunistic overhearing
Native packet	Raw or encoded packets

3.2.1 Necessary Coding Conditions

At first, necessary and sufficient conditions are stated so as to discover paths with potential coding opportunity with the network coding. In this work, the following notations have been incorporated. Let *s* designate a node and N(*s*) indicate the set of one-hop neighbors of node *s*. Further, let F be a flow in which *s* E F to denote that node *s* is along the flow F. Let F_{list} (s,F) represents the set of all forwarding nodes of node s in flow F, and B_{list} (s,F) specifies set of all back warding nodes of node s in flow F. For example in Figure 3.1, F_{listj} (2,F_j)={1}, F_{listj}(3,F_j)={1,2}, F_{listk}(2,F_k)= {7,8,3}, F_{listk} (3,F_k) ={7,8}, B_{listj} (2,F_j)={3,4,5,6}, B_{listj}(3,F_j)={4,5,6} and B_{listk} (2,F_k)={9,10,11}, B_{listk}(3,Fk)={2,9,10,11}. Generally, when two flows say F_j and F_k intersect at a node, say node C, (nodes 2 and 3 in Figure 3.1), packets of these two flows can be encoded for transmission at node 2 and *3 if and only if*, the following coding conditions are met.

The definition of coding conditions is specified as follows:

Coding conditions for two flows, say F_j and F_k, which intersect at node C, are:

- There exists, if (des_j E B_{listj} (C_i)) such that des_j E N(s_k), s_k E F_{listk}(C_i) or des_j E F_{listk}(C_i).
- There exists, if (des_k E B_{listk} (C_i)) such that des_k E N(s_j), s_j E F_{listj}(C_i) or des_k E F_{listj}(C_i).

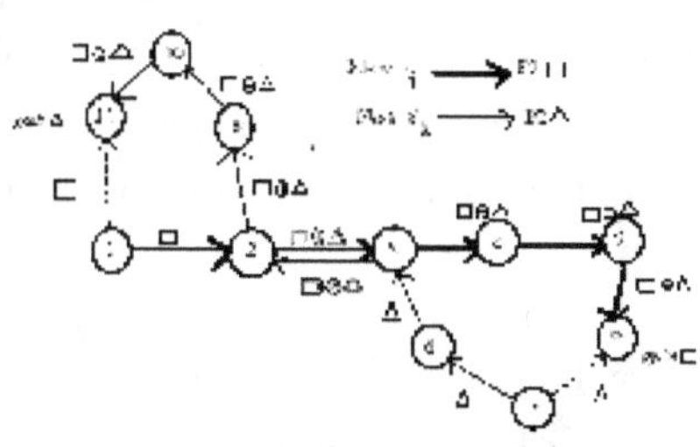

Figure 3.1 Conceptual view of OEDAR algorithm

Lemma 1: The above mentioned conditions are the necessary and sufficient conditions for any appropriate coding and decoding which occur for ideal channel conditions and scheduling (eg. no packet loss or collision).

Proof: To ensure that the destinations of both the flows get their respective "native" packets, there must exist some downstream nodes (i.e. (des_j E B_{listj} (C_i)) and (des_k E B_{listk} (C_i))) which can extract the "native" packets included in the encoded one. For example, in Figure 3.1, it is seen 6 E B_{listj} (3) such that 6 E N (7) and 6 E F_{listk} (3). Without loss of generality, let us consider des_j. It must have P2, before it receives the encoded P1 *EB* P2, and there are only two ways for des_j to obtain P2: either by the fact that des_j can overhear the transmission of P2 by some node in F_{listk}(C_i) (i.e. des_j E N(s_k), s_k E F_{listk}(C_i)), or by the fact that des_j itself transmits P2(i.e., des_j E F_{listk}(C_i). Without these, d1 cannot extract P1 out of the encoded packet. This proves the necessity of the coding conditions. On the other hand, assuming perfect channel condition and scheduling, either way can let des_j receives P2 before it receives the encoded packet. Therefore, it proves the sufficiency of the coding conditions.

For the n native packets p_1, which comes from the flow $F_{j,}$ intersect node C generates the encoded packets p_1 *EB* p_2 and the perfect coding is possible if only if the back warding list of intersect node C on flow j should be the neighborhood of forwarding list of the intersect node on flow k. Also, for the n native packets p_2 which comes from the flow $F_{k,}$ node C generates the encoded packets p_1 *EB* p_2 and the coding is possible only if the back warding list of intersect node C on flow k must be the forwarding list of the intersect node on flow j.

Note: Back warding list of intersect node C on flow j has to be close to the destination on flow j and back warding list of intersect node C on flow k has to be close to the destination on flow k.

Remark: It is necessary to point out that in order to obtain above coding conditions, perfect channel condition and scheduling have been assumed. Due to that fact, some opportunistic overhearing may be failed owing to the channel fading or packet collision at the link layer. Because of that, neighboring nodes with high probability of overhearing (> 0.8) in the coding judgment has been chosen. Prior to network coding, the coding node must ensure whether the encoded flow is decodable which means at least one node in the backward list can be able to decode this encoded flow. To ensure this, the coding node must have the decoding knowledge before taking any coding decision. In interflow network coding, decoding knowledge is referred as the flow's overheard information defined by a group of possible nodes which have or overheard the same flow and it can be obtained by learning neighbor state method for the above coding conditions satisfied, Then, two intersect node have been selected for that flows for the encoding of native packets. At the same time, the corresponding intersect node should satisfy the coding conditions and should be within two-hop region.

CODING AND ROUTE DISCOVERY PROCESS

When a new flow arrives the wireless network, the source node of this new flow activates the *coding and routing discovery process* which has the following steps:

The source node s initiates the route discovery by broadcasting the Route Request (RREQ) message. The RREQ contains one hop neighbors and link qualities. This is to inform intermediate nodes to overhear information along the path. Upon receiving a RREQ, intermediate node, first checks whether the RREQ has already traversed through itself. If so, intermediate node discards the RREQ to prevent loop. Each node temporally stores RREQs during the discovery phase.

When an RREQ reaches the destination node, the destination replies with the Route Reply (RREP) message using the reverse path back to the source node. The RREP is a unicast message that contains the "path" information. Upon receiving a RREP, intermediate node, compares the upstream path contained in the RREP with the paths in its temporally stored RREQs. If there is a match, then it obtains both the "*path*" and "*who-can overhear*" information for the new path. Each node also maintains the "path" and "who-can-overhear" information for all the existing flows relayed by it. From the above information, possible encoding nodes (where it's placed in two-hop region from the first intermediate encoding node) can check whether the new flow can be encoded with some existing flow(s) using the coding conditions. In OEDAR, for selecting a high throughput path with more potential coding opportunities by introducing a coding aware routing metrics anypath cost and delay jointly consider coding opportunities and related factors for comparing coding possible and coding impossible routes, when multiple routes are available.

If there is a best possible coding opportunity, encoded node based on the Optimal Encoder Selection algorithm (OES) marks its link as "coding possible" in the RREP.

When the RREP(s) return to the source node, a routing decision is made based on the potential coding opportunities and the benefit of each available path and the source node begins to send data packets on the selected path. When the first data packet reaches an optimal encoded node C, it stores the "who-can-overhear" and "path" information for the selected path, while discarding other temporarily stored information. Hence, the metric used in OEDAR is of great importance to the formulation of this work.

CALCULATIONS OF ROUTE METRICS

Anypath Cost:

In classic wireless network routing, each node forwards a packet to a single next hop. As a result, if the transmission to that next hop fails, the node needs to retransmit the packet, even though other neighbors may have overheard it. In contrast, in anypath routing, each node broadcasts a packet to multiple next hops simultaneously. Therefore, if the transmission to one neighbor fails, an alternative neighbor who receives the packet, can forward it on. This set of multiple next hops is defined as the forwarding set and J is to represent it throughout the work. A different forwarding set is used to reach each destination and in the same way, a distinct next hop is used for each destination in classic routing. When a packet is broadcast to the forwarding set, more than one node may receive the same packet. To avoid unnecessary duplicate forwarding, only one of these nodes should forward the packet. For this purpose, each node in the set has a priority in relaying the received packet. A node forwards a packet only if all higher priority nodes in the set have failed to do so. Higher priorities are assigned to nodes with shorter distances to the destination (Seferoglu et al 2010). As a result, if the node with the shortest distance in the forwarding set successfully receives the packet, it forwards the packet to the destination while others suppress their transmission. Otherwise, the node with the second shortest distance forwards the packet, and so on (Dubois *et al*, 2007). The source keeps rebroadcasting the packet until someone in the forwarding set receives it or a threshold is reached. Once a neighbor in the set receives the packet, this neighbor repeats the same procedure until the packet is delivered to the destination. Now, a set of next hops is used to forward packets. Every two nodes will be connected through a mesh composed of the union of multiple paths. Figure 3.2 depicts this scenario where each node uses a set of neighbors to forward packets. The forwarding sets are defined by the multiple bold arrows leaving each node. This union of paths between two nodes is defined as an anypath. In the Figure 3.2, the anypath shown in bold is composed by the union of 11 different paths between a source S and a destination D. Depending on the choice of each forwarding set, different paths are included or excluded from the anypath. At every hop, only a single node of the set forwards the packet. Consequently, every packet from *S* traverses only one of the available paths to reach D. The path possibly taken by a packet is shown using the dashed line. Succeeding packets, however, may take completely different paths and hence, t is named as anypath. The path taken is determined on-the-fly, depending on which nodes of the forwarding sets successfully receive the packet at each hop(Jacek &Rak, 2014).

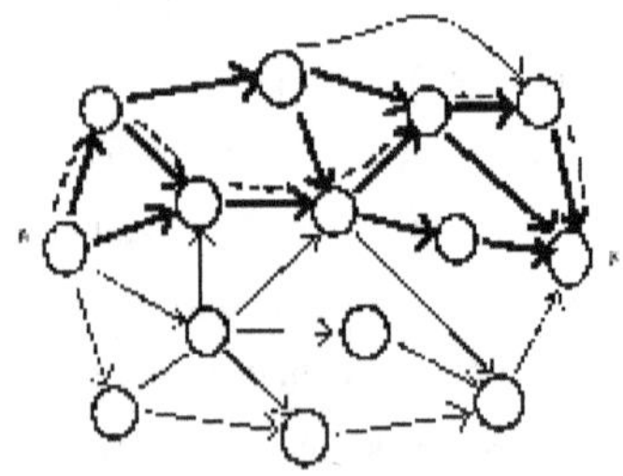

Figure 3.2 Anypath connecting nodes S and D

Anypath is composed of the union of 11 paths between the two nodes S and D and it is shown in Figure 3.2 using bold arrows. Every packet sent from S traverses one of these paths to reach D. Different packets may traverse different paths, depending on which nodes receive the forwarded packet at each hop with higher priority named as anypath and it is shown in dashed line in Figure 3.2(Rafael et al 2009).

In order to support the point -to- multipoint links used in anypath routing in Figure 3.3 , the wireless mesh network is represented as a hyper graph G= (V, E), where V is the set of nodes, and E is the set of hyperlinks,

Each hyperlink is being an ordered pair (i,J), where i is a given node connected with the forwarding set J of neighboring node. The cost of anypath from a given node i to the destination D via a forwarding set J is defined using Bellman equation:

$$C_i = C_{iJ} + C_J \tag{3.1}$$

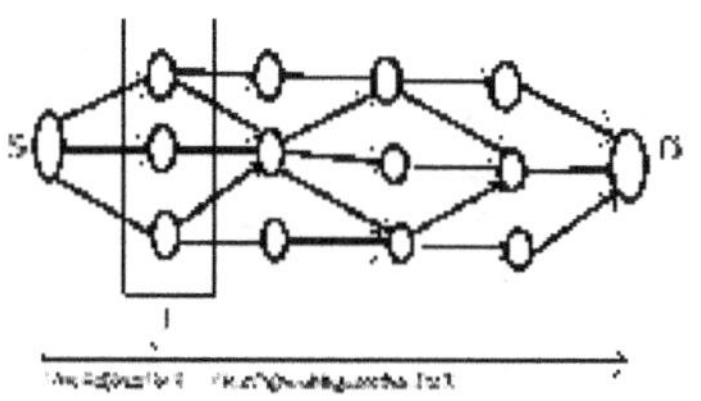

Figure 3.3 Scheme of anypath cost calculation

This is composed of the broadcast cost C_{iJ} from i to J and the remaining-anypath cost C_J from J to the destination. Assuming independent packet losses, C_{iJ} can be defined as:

$$C_{ij} = \frac{1}{d_{ij}} = \frac{1}{1 - \prod_{j \in J}(1 - d_{ij})} \tag{3.2}$$

where d_{iJ} is the probability of packet delivery from node *i* to at least one node from J based on the individual probabilities of packet delivery d_{ij} for links (i, j). C_{iJ} value represents the Expected number of Anypath Transmission (EATX) needed to successfully deliver the packet sent by node i to any node from J. EATX is a generalization of the unidirectional ETX metric. Remaining cost C_J is defined as the weighted *average* costs of all paths from J to D,

$$C_J = \sum_{j \in J} w_{ij} \, C_j \text{, with} \sum_{j \in J} w_j = 1 \qquad (3.3)$$

where C_j is the cost of a path between a node j from J and the destination node D, while weight w_{ij} in equation (3.3) denotes probability of node j being the forwarding node of a packet received from node i. The weight w_{ij} is then defined as

$$w_{ij} = \frac{d_{ij} \prod_{k=1}^{j-1} (1 - d_{ik})}{1 - \prod_{j \in J} (1 - d_{ij})} \tag{3.4}$$

Among all possible paths, the anypath is selected based on the shortest Expected Transmission Count (ETX). In any path routing, an intermediate node receives a packet from a flow only when the destination and neighbours should be in the downstream of this flow. According to the coding condition, the potential decoding nodes of this packet should be either in destination or in one hop before the destination.

Delay

Delay is expressed to be the difference of time at which the sender produces the packet and the time at which the receiver gets the packet. In various networking applications, delay plays a vital role in analyzing the performance metric along with throughput. In addition, throughput obtained from a network at the cost of increasing delay might not be useful. Due to this, understanding of throughput-delay trade-off is a key to obtain the quality of service desired by the application. Many existing works have emphasized only on obtaining the highest throughput with no intention of decreasing delay or the trade-off between throughput and delay.

Delay of OEDAR algorithmz

End-to-End delay = L (arrive time - send time) I L Number of connections (3.5)

The objective function for delay can be expressed as follows:

$$f_1 = min\ L\ D_{ij}X_{ij}$$
$$(i,jE\ E)$$

Dij - delay between the link (i, j)

Xij - The particular link (i , j) is considered in the routing path or not.

Virtual Flow List

Whenever a flow passes any node, details of that node and flow are being maintained as virtual flow list in OEDAR so that *source* and *destination* recognize a flow uniquely. Potential encoded flow or encoding status is marked by *coding flag*. The status of expiry of this flow is being represented by *coding expire* and the dynamic list of forwarding set of the encoded flow is expressed by the *forwarding list flag* which has any path cost of every potential next hop. It is set to zero, if no network coding occurs. Virtual flow is generated from the virtual flow list whenever a node gets the first packet from a new flow there by, all other following packets from the same flow get triggered an update of this virtual flow. Two different updates are being used for a virtual flow in OEDAR, one is *regular update* that is triggered by each packet received from the native flow in which only *expire flag* will be reset. The other is *coding update* which starts only after getting an ACK packet from the coding node. When *coding flag* is set to 1, *coding expire* will be reset, and the forwarding list will be changed respectively. Every node will maintain the timer to refresh virtual flow list and hence, it will be deleted, once it is expired. The *coding flag* is set to zero, if this virtual flow is not being proceeded as an encoded flow.

ALGORITHM FOR OPTIMAL ENCODER SELECTION

The coding procedure algorithm illustrated is executed, when a node *i* receives a new packet p_k from flow f_k.

Algorithm for optimal Encoder Selection

```
II Fj, Fk - Input flow list
II Flistj, Flistk - Collection of forwarder list of each node in the flow Fj andFk
II Blistj ,Blistk- Collection of backwarder list of each node in the flow Fj and Fk
II CNjk- list of common node of flow Fj and Fk
II dstj, dstk - destination node of flow j and k

Input : Flows Fj, Fk, Flistj, Flistk, Blistj, BlistK, dstj, dstk, CNjk;
        Begin
         if Fj == 0  &Fk == 0 then
                return No_Route;
        end if
         set Cn ←  0;
        for each Ci E CNjk
        {
check if coding possible (Ci)
estimate cost Ci using equation (3.1);
estimate delay Ci using equation (3.5);
        if Cn == 0
            {
        PcostCi ← CostCi;
        PdelayCi ← delayCi;
optimal encoder en ← Ci;
            }
        else
          {
        if (CostCi<= PcostCi)&&(delay Ci<= PdelayCi)&&(Ci belongs to two hop of Cn))
                {  optimal encoder ← enCi;
                PcostCiCost ← Ci;
                PdelayCi ← delayCi;
                } } }
                End
```

Algorithm for coding possible node (C_i)

```
begin
        coding j =0;
        coding k= 0;
        if (B_listj (C_i) E N(F_listk (C_i))where B_listj(C_i) near to dst_j;
                decoding j = B_listj(C_i);
                O_j = N(F_listk (C_i));
                Coding j =1;
        endif
        if (B_listk (C_i) E N(F_listj(C_i))where B_listk(C_i) near to dst_k;
                decoding k =B_listk(C_i) ;
                O_k = N(F_listj (C_i));
                Coding k =1;
        endif
        return (coding j * coding k);
end.
```

Lines 4 and 9 in above algorithm entails the coding condition and lemma 1. The cost and delay obey the Equations 3.1 and 3.5 in which any path cost has been employed for network coding. Network coding can be done only if decoding node is being the destination for each virtual flow list. When network coding is done at node i after passing 'n' encoded packets over a period of time, CK is sent back from i to the preceding hop of destination and this kind of feedback is known as *coding feedback.* In OEDAR, control header of coding feedback has four attributes: *src, dst, cost* and *delay* in which source and destination of the flow p_k are identified by *src* and *dst.* The *cost* and *delay* are utilized for performing delay and any path cost calculation in network coding. After sending coding feedback to neighbor of i, the virtual flow list gets updated, and based on its updating, the next hops stored in the virtual flow list tend to become more competitive to gain high priority to forward this packet. If the network coding departs, virtual flow will not be updated. After it gets expiration, virtual flow list will be destroyed and then, new packet would be forwarded after existing any path cost.

Decoding

In OEDAR, every node keeps track of all packets sent andoverheard by itself, during the past T seconds in the *packet pool*. The decoding process occurs after the encoded packet reaches at a node and the address of this node is present in the decoding(Zhou et al, 2011). As XOR coding method is being used, the encoded packet could be decoded only by performing XOR of the virtual native (un-coded) packets such as $p1 = (p1\ EB\ p2)\ EB\ p2$.

SIMULATION ENVIRONMENT AND PERFORMANCE EVALUATION

This work has been implemented in NS-2 simulator. NS-2 simulator is a discrete event simulator, mostly used in networking. This simulator is based on a split-object model. The simulation code is written in OTcl language and most logic can be executed in C or C++. The performance of OEDAR is compared with HCOR algorithm in random and grid topologies. NS-2 Simulators revise a problem at number of different levels of abstraction. By approaching a system at a high level of construct, it realizes the performance and communications of all components of the system and it is also equipped to counter the system's complexity. A simulation process using NS-2 simulator is a low-cost compared to a real-time implementation. Predominantly, all the tests may have to be carried out repeatedly using different parts to reach the objective. Using simulators, it is possible to compare alternative design and select the optimal system. The performance of the proposed algorithm OEDAR is tested in several scenarios. In the simulation, 100 mobile nodes are placed randomly in an area of 1000m x 1000m. The performance of OEDAR is compared with the existing HCOR coding scheme. The NC scheme, HCOR which is a sort of coding opportunity-aware Opportunity Routing method running on a multihop coding structure. The major difference between HCOR and OEDAR is that HCOR performs the network coding whenever a coding opportunity occurs and the first node would be chosen among the coding nodes, where as OEDAR does not select the first coding node from the coding opportunity, instead, the node which has more gain and minimum delay among the coding nodes would be chosen as the coding node. In OEDAR, all the nodes are connected with promiscuous mode in order to save all packets for further analysis with a customized IEEE 802.11 standard as the MAC protocol which carries the opportunistic transmission. User Datagram Protocol (UDP) has been utilized as traffic sources, and all the flows are set to fixed packet size of 512 bytes as Constant Bit Rate (CBR). The transmission range is kept as 250 m, and the interference range is set to 550 m by using Two Ray Ground propagation model.

Simulation Result and Analysis

In this simulation, when compared with the existing High throughput code aware routing algorithm, the proposed OEDAR routing algorithm with optimal encoder node is effective in terms of performance metrics such as throughput, end- to -end delay, packet delivery ratio. The simulation is performed with 100,300 and 500 nodes. The proposed path selection algorithm takes the anypath cost and delay into account and selects reliable encoded path by using coding conditions and OES algorithm to estimate the performance. The performance metrics are obtained by calculating the average result of 20 test runs. The Table 3.2 shows the performance comparison of the proposed OEDAR routing algorithm using network coding for various parameters with the existing HCOR routing algorithm (Long *et al.* 2014). The gain obtained by OEDAR appears to be larger with higher offered load when number of flow increases, OEDAR generates more coding opportunities by "coding+routing" options than HCOR.

Time complexity and processing time

Amount of time taken by a set of code or algorithm to process or run as a function of the amt of input.

Time Complexity: O(abc)

Where a is the number of encoding node in j^{th} flow

b is the number of encoding node in k^{th} flow

c is the number of links

Notably, the transmission of packets from each source node starts exactly at simulation period of about 10 s and the transmission is continued till the simulation time reaches to 100 s.

Table 3.2 Performance Comparison Metrics for 100 nodes

S.No	Offered load (kbs)	Throughput (kbps)				Packet Delivery Ratio			
		Random Topology		Grid Topology		Random Topology		Grid Topolog	
		HCOR	OEDAR	HCOR	OEDAR	HCOR	OEDAR	HCOR	OEDA
1	150	89.942	99.956	108.563	115.705	81.6667	90.9091	89.4359	97.80
2	300	89.994	111.421	101.721	113.10	82.8947	92.8571	90.5904	98.61
3	450	88.273	111.721	100.907	110.453	82.0513	92.5714	91.8254	98.428
4	600	87.725	112.725	100.64	110.845	81.7797	92.8839	92.127	98.467

Table 3.3 Performance Comparison Metrics for 300 nodes

S.No	Offered load (kbs)	Throughput (kbps)				Packet Delivery Ratio		
		Random Topology		Grid Topology		Random Topology		Grid T
		HCOR	OEDAR	HCOR	OEDAR	HCOR	OEDAR	HCOR
1	150	98.539	103.954	112.905	120.333	84.926	94.545	93.013
2	300	93.593	115.876	105.788	117.624	84.894	94.001	92.591
3	450	91.804	116.19	104.943	114.871	84.053	93.561	93.826
4	600	91.234	117.234	104.66	115.278	83.86	95.001	93.316

Table 3.4 Performance Comparison Metrics for 500 nodes

S.No	Offered load (kbs)	Throughput (kbps)				Packet Delivery Ratio			
		Random Topology		Grid Topology		Random Topology		Grid Topology	
		HCOR	OEDAR	HCOR	OEDAR	HCOR	OEDAR	HCOR	OEDAR
1	150	97.1373	107.958	117.248	124.961	80.66	88.909	86.435	92.805
2	300	97.19352	120.337	110.338	122.148	80.894	89.85	85.590	91.619
3	450	95.33484	120.657	108.979	119.289	79.051	88.571	84.825	90.4286
4	600	94.32	115.123	107.71	109.289	75.058	78.537	79.12	85.430

Throughput

Throughput is one of the important parameters for evaluating the performance. The throughput is calculated based on number of bits transmitted per second. The performance of OEDAR has been analyzed in a larger random mesh network in which 100, 300 and 500 nodes with size 1,000 x 1,000 have been constructed. Moreover, 5 by 5 grid topology has been constructed where each node can reach its surrounding neighboring nodes and the experiments have been conducted over 100,300 and 500 nodes for 20 rounds. At every round, 5 flows are added randomly into the network and the same process is repeated for 3 times. The Table 3.2, 3.3 and 3.4 shows the performance comparison of the existing high throughput code aware routing algorithm and proposed ODEAR routing algorithm based on transmission rate for random topology and grid topology.

It is analyzed from the Figure 3.4 and Figure 3.5, that the throughput for the 100 nodes for the proposed ODEAR is gradually increasing compared to the existing high throughput code aware routing algorithm. In the proposed ODEAR, the best coding opportunity paths are selected using optimal encoder algorithm based on anypath cost and delay. Therefore, the proposed OEDAR gives better throughput using network coding in wireless mesh networks.

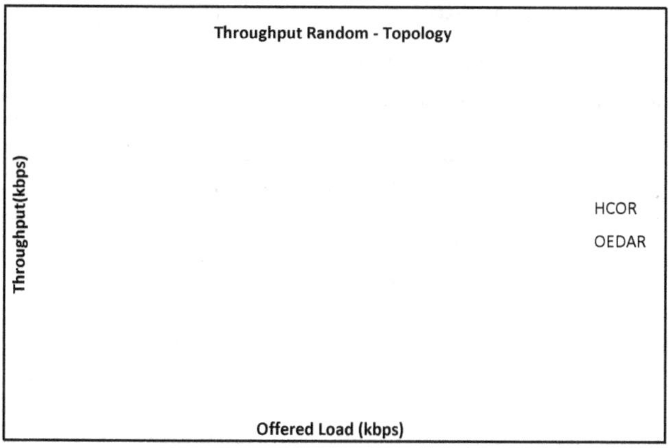

Figure 3.4 Throughput of OEDAR and HCOR for random topology

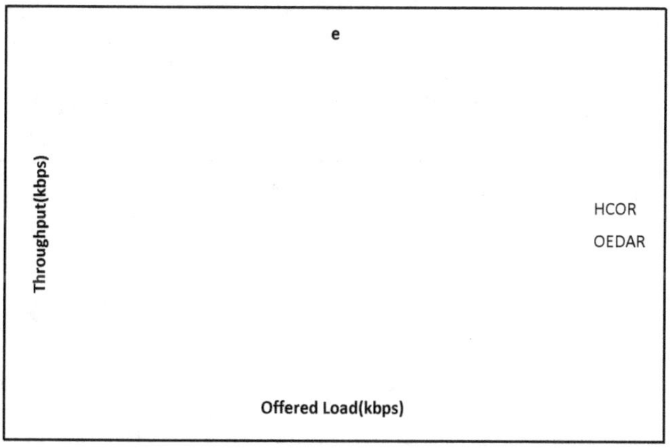

Figure 3.5 Throughput of OEDAR and HCOR for grid topology

End-to-End delay

The ratio of packet received time to the packet sent time is termed as end-to-end delay. The end-to-end delay should be low in order to provide better performance. The Figure3.6 and Figure 3.7 show the performance graphs of routing end-to-end delay in continuous traffic pattern for HCOR and OEDAR routing algorithms for random and grid topologies for 100 nodes.

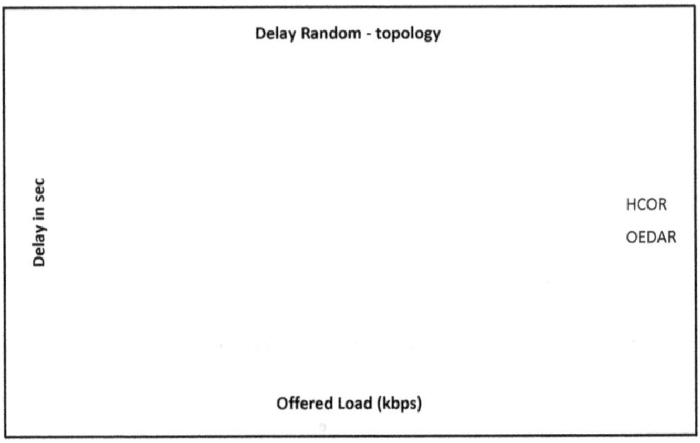

Figure 3.6 Delay of OEDAR and HCOR for random topology

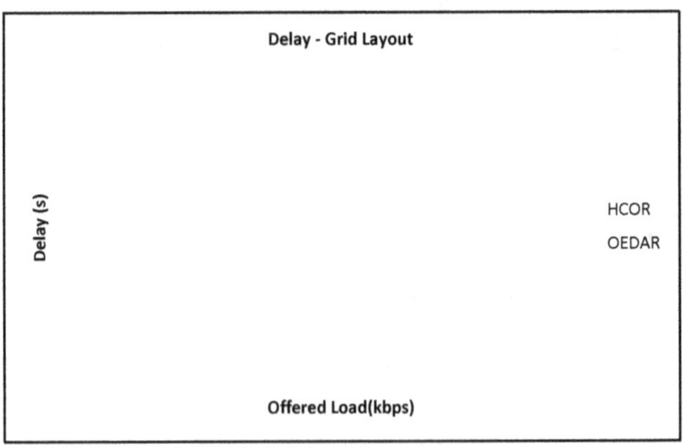

Figure 3.7 Delay of OEDAR and HCOR for grid topology

In this proposed OEDAR, due to the optimal encoder selection algorithm, the best encoder node is selected among all the possible encoding nodes with two hop region based on the route metrics i.e. anypath cost and delay. Based on the factors, OEDAR selects the best routing path from the source to the destination and because of that, the packet can be delivered within time while increasing the speed. Thus, the proposed OEDAR performs better with low end-to-end delay compared to the existing HCOR routing algorithm.

Packet Delivery Ratio

Packet Delivery Ratio (PDR) is defined as the ratio between the total numbers of packet send and the total number of packets received.PDR for a path is the sum of the PDR links along the path from the source to the sink. The performance graphs for 100 nodes in Figure 3.8 and Figure 3.9 represent the routing packet delivery ratio of the existing HCOR algorithm and the proposed OEDAR algorithm with respect to speed for random and grid topologies. Due to the optimal path selection using anypath cost, the best coding opportunity paths have been selected by the proposed OEDAR. Thus, there is the possibility to receive more packets without any loss. The proposed OEDAR algorithm achieves high packet delivery ratio than the existing HOR algorithm and it gives better result.

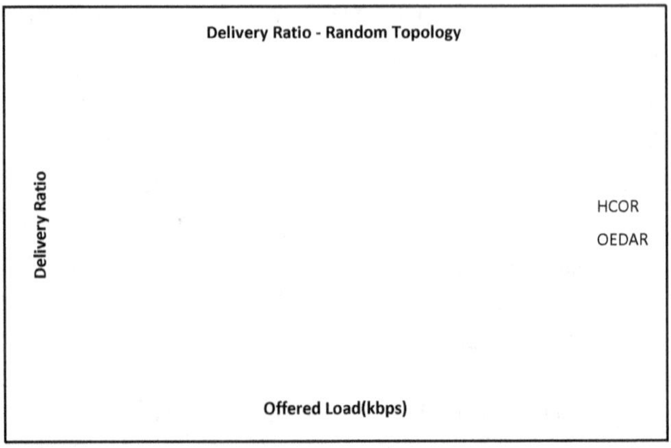

Figure 3.8 Packet Delivery Ratio of OEDAR and HCOR for random topology

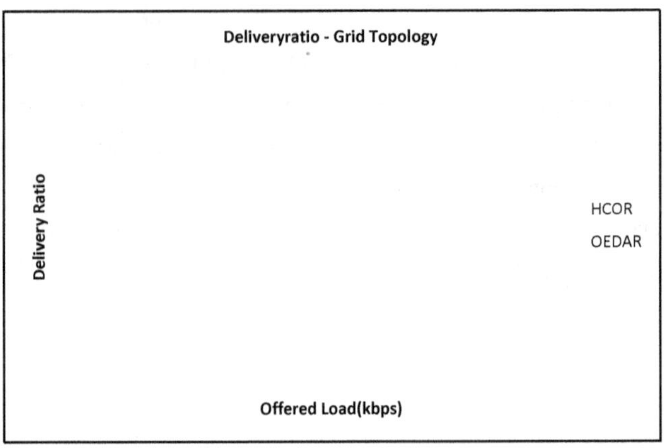

Figure 3.9 Packet Delivery Ratio of OEDAR and HCOR for grid topology

SUMMARY

In this chapter, a novel coding-aware opportunistic routing scheme OEDAR has been proposed to learn the characteristics of employing NC into opportunistic routing there by figuring out some conclusions for designing a coding-aware opportunistic routing. Potential and optimal coding has been utilized for the consideration of route selection in OEDAR and it has multi hop coding structure. OEDAR has been incorporated to the Optimal Encoder Selector [OES] algorithm so as to maximize the throughput and minimizing the delay. By establishing optimal encoder selection algorithm and any path cost, a computing method is constructed to calculate the network coding cost in opportunistic transmission. Based on the above study, a distributed routing scheme has been designed to realize OEDAR, which regards the multihop coding structure in the design. In addition to this, high packet delivery ratio is achieved where as the overhead in not increased significantly.

CHAPTER 4

ADAPTIVE CODING AWARE ROUTING ALGORITHM IN WIRELESS MESH NETWORKS (ACAR)

The majority of coding aware routing schemes centres on maximizing the coding opportunities. This chapter emphasizes the benefits of network coding in the opportunistic routing. An Adaptive Coding Aware Routing Algorithm (ACAR) has been proposed to encode the packets in two different flows that will not have the intermediate nodes. In this algorithm, route metrics are used to quantify the merits of the routes. The performance evaluation of ACAR algorithm significantly improves the throughput in network topologies.

OVERVIEW

When a new flow arrives the wireless mesh network, the source node of this new flow activates the *coding and routing discovery process* as same as OEDAR routing algorithm. Route has been discovered by using Route REQuest message (RREQ) which is broadcasted by the source node. Each intermediate node temporarily stores RREQs during the discovery phase. The destination node receives the RREQ, and then, it replies with the Route Reply (RREP) message using the reverse path back to the source node. Upon getting an RREP, an intermediate node is compared and matched up to the upstream path contained in the RREP with the paths in its temporarily stored RREQs. If there is a match, then it obtains both the *'path'* and *'who-can overhear'* information for the new flow. Each node in the routing path also maintains the 'path' and 'who-can-overhear' information for all the existing flows relayed by itself. If the two flows don't have the intermediate nodes, then the existing flows collect the overhear information of the other flow. If any node has the same neighbouring nodes in their forwarder list, then that particular node has to be selected as an intermediate node for two distinct flows. Flow Adaptive Code Aware Routing Algorithm(F-ACAR) selects the optimal and adaptive encoder node from any one of the distinct flow and Selective flow Adaptive Code aware Routing (S-ACAR) algorithm selects any node which will be the neighboring of the forwarding nodes of two distinct flows based on the anypath cost, delay and bandwidth estimation metrics. Due to this estimation, ACAR is able to identify the high throughput path with more coding opportunities and high packet delivery paths. ACAR jointly considers coding opportunities and related factors for comparing coding possible and coding impossible routes, when multiple routes are available. Hence, the metric used in ACAR is of great importance to the formulation of this chapter.

Flow - Adaptive Code Aware Routing Algorithm (F-ACAR)

In network coding, the coding possible is applicable, when two flows have the common intersecting node. If two flows don't have the intersecting node but have the common overhearing node for any one of the flow, F-ACAR algorithm can be used to do the network coding to reduce the number of transmission and increase the throughput. At first, the underlying assumptions used in this article are stated. A 'coding node' is referred as a node which encodes packets such as node 2 or 3 or 6 or 7 as in Figure 4.1. A 'coding structure' is a collection of nodes and flows including the necessary transmitters for opportunistic overhearing, the coding node, the intended receivers which decode packets, and the necessary relaying nodes connecting the flows. The examples include all the structures of Figure 4.1. Coding structures are considered to be the basic building blocks for general networks which use the network coding paradigm. Throughout this work, the interflow coding fashion is emphasized similar to the ones used in DCAR

(Le *et al.* 2010). The central idea is to ensure that every encoded packet should be decoded by the respective receiver.

4.2.1 Necessary Coding Conditions

Necessary and sufficient conditions to discover the paths with potential coding opportunity using network coding are stated below. The following notations have been incorporated. Let s designate a node and N(s) indicate the set of one-hop neighbors of node s. Further, let F be a flow in which s E F to denote that node s is along the flow F. Let F_{list} (s,F) represents the set of all forwarding nodes of node s in flow F, and B_{list} (s,F) specifies set of all back warding nodes of node s in flow F. For example in Figure 4.1, F_{listA} (2,F_A)={1},F_{listA}(3,F_j)={1,2}, F_{listB}(6,F_B)= {8,7},F_{listB} (7,F_B) ={8}, B_{listA} (2,F_j)={3,4},B_{listA}(3,F_A)={4}, B_{listB} (6,F_k)={1}, B_{listk}(7,Fk)={6,1}. Generally, when two flows say F_A and F_B don't have intersect node, say node C, (nodes 2 and 6 in Figure 4.1), packets of these two flows can be encoded for transmission at nodes 2 and 6 *if and only if* the following coding conditions are met.

The definition of coding conditions is specified as follows:

Definition 1 (coding condition): coding conditions for two flows, say F_A and F_B, which have encoded node C, are:

- There exists, if (B_{listA} (C_A) E N(F_{listB} (C_B)) where B_{listA}(C_i) near to dst_A
- There exists, if (B_{listB} (C_i) E N(F_{listA}(C_i)) where B_{listB}(C_i) near to dst_k

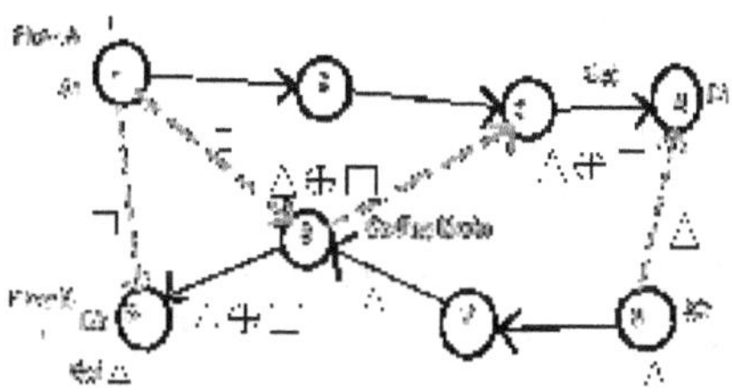

Figure 4.1 Network coding of two neighboring flows without having the intermediate node

In Figure 4.1, there are two flows A and B. Flow A is 1→2→ 3→4 and flow B is 8→ 7→ 6→5. The above flows don't have any intersection node for doing network coding. But, flow A has the overhearing nodes (6 or 7) in flow B, at the same time, flow B(2 or 3) has the overhearing nodes list in flow A. With the arrival of a new flow B, new coding opportunities are introduced at nodes 6 and 7. These two nodes can sense this new opportunity as an intermediate node.

Without the knowledge of forwarders and backwards list of two flows, Flow A will not be aware of the flow arrival B and also does not mention changing the route to utilize this coding opportunity. In F-ACAR protocol, flow A changes the route via 1→ 6→ 3 →4 or 1→2→7→4 based on the optimal encoder node and by fully utilizing the coding opportunity. Without network coding to transmit the packets from node 1 to 4, 3 transmissions (1→2→3→4) are required, at the same time to transmit the packets from node 8 to 5, 3 transmissions (8→7→6→5) are required. So totally 6 transmissions are required for flow A and B. Using network coding, if node 6 is selected as a encoded node, then the transmission will be 1→6→3→4 and 8→7→6→5. Here, the encoded node 6, code the packets using XOR function and broadcast the packets from node 1 from flow A and 7 from flow B, so that only 5 transmissions are required instead of 6 transmissions.

SELECTIVE FLOW- ADAPTIVE CODE AWARE ROUTING ALGORITHM (S-ACAR)

If the two flows don't have the common intersecting node or common overhearing node in the forwarders and backwards list of any one flow, then S-ACAR algorithm is to be selected to do the network coding. S-ACAR algorithm is applicable only when two flows have common overhearing node in the network. Then, any one of the optimal node has to be selected and that should be placed in neighbor list of two flows. It should also satisfy the coding condition i.e destination of flow A should be listed in forwarder list of flow B and destination of flow B should be listed in forwarder list of flow A.

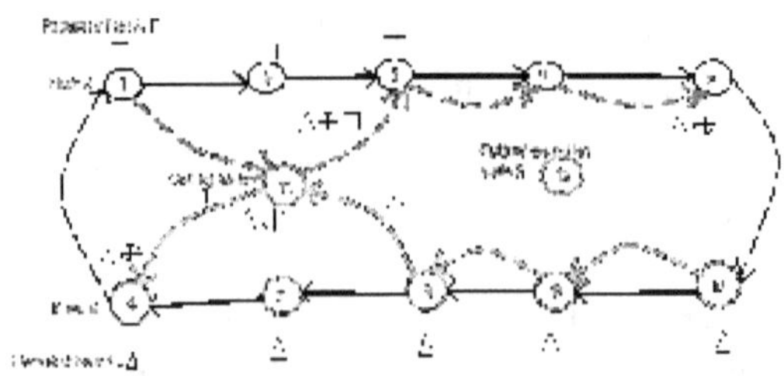

Figure 4.2 Network coding of two different flows not having the intermediate node and not having the common neighbouring node in any one of the two flows.

For the above example in Figure 4.2, two distinct flows are taken. Flow A needs 4 transmissions to deliver the packet from node 1 to 5 (1➔2➔3➔4➔5) and at the same time, flow B requires 4 transmissions to deliver the packet from node 10 to 6 (10➔9➔8➔7➔6). Hence, totally 8 transmissions are required for two flows. In Figure 4.2, node 11 and 12are considered and both the nodes are common opportunistic node of two flows A and B. Using node 11, flow A and flow B reroute the routing procedure via 1➔11➔ 3➔4➔5 and 10➔9➔8➔11➔6. In this, node 11 XORed and broadcasts the packets from node 1 and 8 Because of that, three transmissions have to be reduced instead of four transmissions. The reduction oftransmission time of both the flows can increase the throughput. Using the optimal encoder selection algorithm, another route has to be selected for flow A i.e. 1→2→3→12→5 and for flow B i.e. 10→12→8→7→6. To utilize the coding opportunity, severe problems have to be faced based on the reroute procedure. The first is discovering of new flows and new coding opportunities. The second one is evaluation of these coding opportunities and taking decision of changing the existing routes. To complete the procedure, a third step is also done to test whether the newly introduced complexity is well compensated with high performance.

CALCULATIONS OF ROUTE METRICS

Anypath Cost

Traditional Routing protocols for wireless networks are focused to find the best path for forwarding packets between a pair of nodes. S*ingle-path* forwarding is suitable for wired networks with relatively stable point-to-point links, where as it is not suitable for wireless networks with broadcast links of time varying qualities. Fluctuations in the quality of any of the links along the predetermined single path can create unnecessary retransmissions at the link layer or re-routings at the network layer. Consequently, *opportunistic* routing technique, that alleviates the impact of link quality variations by exploiting the broadcast nature of wireless transmissions is actively explored (Biswas & morries, 2003, Sanjit Zubin & iswas 2005, Romit *et al.* 2004). A set of candidate next-hops has been selected by each destination in-advance and one of them is selected for forwarding a per-packet basis according to its reachability at that instant. By employing such *opportunistic forwarding*, these techniques reduce the number of transmissions needed for reliable delivery of a packet to its destination.

Different packets may traverse different paths, depending on which nodes receive the forwarded packet at each hop with higher priority named as anypath. In order to support the point -to- multipoint links used in anypath routing(figure 4.3), the wireless mesh network is represented as a hypergraph G=(V,E), where V is the set of nodes consisting of both mesh client and mesh routers and E is the set of edges representing wireless links between the nodes. A path from node V_i to node V_j is the sequence of nodes from V in which no node appears more than once. Each hyperlink is an ordered pair (i,J), where i is a given node connected with the forwarding set J of neighboring node. The cost of anypath from a given node i to the destination D via a forwarding set J defined using Bellman equation is referred in chapter 3.4.1.

Among all the possible paths, the anypath cost route metric: *Expected Any-path Transmission* (EAX) is selected based on the shortest Expected Transmission Count(ETX). ETX metric gets the effect of both the path length and packet loss ratio. EAX route metric for a pair of nodes with a given set of candidates captures the expected number of transmissions between them under opportunistic forwarding. Using this EAX metric, ACAR algorithm selects candidates which really contribute to packet delivery and it correctly prioritizes the candidates from the forwarding set of node. It provides less computation of the smallest weight paths and loop free paths. The main objective of ACAR algorithm is to select high throughput path without any packet losses.

In any path routing, an intermediate node receives a packet from a flow only when the destination and neighbours should be in the downstream of this flow. According to the coding condition (Definition 1), the potential decoding nodes of this packet should be either in destination or in one hop before the destination.

End-to-End Delay

The End-to-End delay is the sum of the delay of links along the path from the source to the destination. The End-to-End delay is the average time taken by a data packet to arrive the destination (Mallapur et al, 2010). It also includes the delay caused by route discovery process and the queue in data packet transmission. Only the data packets that are successfully delivered to destinations are counted. End-to- end delay considers the transmission delay, queuing delay, propagation delay, transfer time and retransmission delay at the MAC. Each node in a flow needs not only to monitor the transmission failure probability to estimate the transmission delay , but also to measure the no of packets waiting in the buffer to evaluate the queuing delay.

The average end to end delay D_i is computed by,

End-to-End delay = **I** (arrive time - send time) / Number of connections

$$D_{i=} \frac{\sum_{i=1}^{n}(R_i - s_i)}{n} \ ms \qquad (4.1)$$

D_i - Average end-to-end delay

n - Number of data packets successfully transmitted over the WMNs

i - Unique packet identifier

Ri - Time at which a packet with unique identifier ' i ' is received

Si - Time at which a packet with unique identifier ' i ' is sent

The Average end-to-end delay is to be less for high performance.

Bandwidth Estimation

Bandwidth Estimation is an important consideration in QoS-aware routing and it is used for supporting real-time video or audio transmission. To support bandwidth-guaranteed QoS, the available bandwidth from source to the destination should be known. Each node estimates its consumed bandwidth by tracking the packets transmitted through the network. This value is recorded in the bandwidth consumption register at the node and it is updated periodically.

Hello Bandwidth Estimation: In the 'Hello' bandwidth estimation method, the sender's current bandwidth usage are well as the sender's one-hop neighbours' current bandwidth usage is piggybacked onto the standard 'Hello' message. Each host estimates its available bandwidth based on the information provided in the 'Hello' messages and knowledge of the frequency reuse pattern. This approach avoids creating extra control messages by using the 'Hello' messages to disseminate the bandwidth information.

ID	Consumed Bandwidth	Timestamp
Neighbor ID 1	Consumed Bandwidth	Timestamp
. . . .	. . . .	. . . .
Neighbor ID n	Consumed Bandwidth	Timestamp

Figure 4.3 Hello Structure

ACAR uses the 'Hello' messages to update the neighbor caches. The 'Hello' message keeps the address of the host who initiates this message. The 'Hello' message is modified to include two fields. The first field includes host address, consumed bandwidth and timestamp and the second field includes neighbor's addresses, consumed bandwidth and timestamp, as shown in Figure

4.3. Each host determines its consumed bandwidth by monitoring the packets that it feeds into the network. This value is recorded in a bandwidth-consumption register at the host and is updated periodically.

$$BW_{ij} = \frac{1}{1-\prod_{j \in J} bw_{ij}} \tag{4.2}$$

where bw_{ij} is a consumed bandwidth for the transmission from i to j.

CODING PROCEDURE AND CODING FEEDBACK

Whenever a node *i* receive a new packet p_k from flow f_k, it executes the coding procedure illustrated in Algorithm 1.

Adaptive Optimal Encoder Coding Condition Algorithm

Algorithm 1 - Adaptive Optimal Encoder coding condition:

// F_j, F_k - Input flow list

// f_j - any node in flow F_j

// f_k - any node in flow F_k

// $Flist_j$, $Flist_k$ - Collection of forwarder list of each node in the flow F_j and F_k

// $Blist_j$,$Blist_k$- Collection of backwarder list of each node in the flow F_j and F_k

// CN_{jk}- list of common node of flow F_j and F_k

// dst_j, dst_k - destination node of flow j and k

Input : F_j, F_k, $Flist_j$, $Flist_k$, $Blist_j$, $Blist_k$, CN_{jk}, dst_j, dst_k,

if ($F_j == <1$ & $F_k == <1$) then

    return "No Route"

else if (common node CN_{jk} is not empty)

    select algorithm 2

else

    No common node for flow F_j & F_k

if (f_j F_j is a neighbor of f_k F_k)

{pick f_j as a common node and put into the CN_{jk}

```
        select algorithm 2
          }
else if (fk∉Fk is a neighbor of fj Fj∉)
    {
        pick fk as common node and put into the CN jk
    select algorithm 2
    }
else
  {
for each node n ∈N; n ∄ Fj & n ∄ Fk
{
if (n is a neighbor of fj Fj∉&& n is a neighbor of backward list of (fj) && n is a
    neighbor of forward list (f j) && n is a neighbor of fk ∉k&& n is a neighbor of
    Blistk(fk) && n is a neighbor of Flistk)
{
put n into CNjk
select algorithm 2
}end
}end
}end
if CNjk is empty
return N -route
else
return Success
endif
```

Optimal Encoder Selection Algorithm

Optimal encoder node selection is based on the weighted average of the each route metrics measured by ACAR routing Algorithm.

```
# Algorithm 2 for optimal Encoder selection:
Input : Fj, Fk, Flistj, Flistk,Blistj, Blistk,dstj, dstk
Common node(Fj, Fk) -+CNjk
If (coding possible (i))
```

```
{
 Estimate cost C_i using equation (3.1)
Estimate delay D_i using equation (4.1)
Estimate bandwidth BW_i using equation (4.2)
}
for each node 'i' in coding possible list
calculate T_j= (W_1C_i +W_2D_i+W_3 BW_i)
find max (T_j)→T_k→k is optimal node
end
 end
```

Selection of coding possible node

Algorithm for the selection of coding possible node based on the coding condition in definition 1 is described below

```
# Algorithm for coding possible node C_i :
Codingj = 0;
Codingk= 0;
if (Blist_j(C_i ) □N(Flist_k(C_i)) where Blist_j(C_i) near to dst_j;
decoding j = Blist_j(C_i);
O_j = N (Flist_k(C_i));
Coding j =1;
end
if (Blist_k(C_i) □N(Flist_j(C_i))where Blist_k(C_i) near to dst_k;
 decoding k =Blist_k(C_i);
O_k = N (F_listj(C_i));
 Coding k =1;
end
 return(Codingj□Codingk);
end
```

4.6 DECODING

In ACAR, every node works in the promiscuous mode and stores all overheard packets in its Packet Pool. The encoded packet can be decoded using XOR method such as $p1 = (p1 \oplus p2) \oplus p2$.

4.7 SIMULATION ENVIRONMENT AND PERFORMANCE EVALUATION

The performances of F-ACAR and S-ACAR are evaluated by comparing with HCOR coding scheme using NS2 Simulator. NS-2 simulation is an application designed to replicate a real-life circumstance. Simulation models have numerous benefits compared to mathematical models and physical experimentation. NS-2 simulator is able to provide users with practical feedback when designing real world environments. Hence, the correctness and efficiency of a design is resolved before the system is really constructed. 100 , 300 and 500 nodes random topologies with size of 1,000m x 1,000m have been constructed. Network coding opportunity-aware routing method, HCOR runs on a multihop coding structure. HCOR does the network coding whenever a coding opportunity occurs and selects the first node among the coding nodes. When F-ACAR and S-ACAR do not select the first coding node from the coding opportunity, it selects the node which has more gain and minimum delay among the coding nodes. In the simulations, all the nodes are set to the promiscuous mode with a modified IEEE 802.11 standard MAC protocol which supports the opportunistic transmission. User Datagram Protocol (UDP) traffic sources are used and all the flows are Constant Bit Rate (CBR), with a fixed packet size of 512 bytes. The transmission range is set to 250 m, and the interference range is set to 550 m with Two Ray Ground propagation model. Multiple runs with different initial values have been conducted for each scenario, and the collected data are averaged over those runs.

Table 4.1 and 4.5 lists the simulation parameters and environments, which are used as default values unless otherwise specified.

Table 4.5 Simulation Parameters

Parameters	Values	
	TCP/FTP	**UDP/CBR**
Traffic Agent Type	FTP	CBR
Data Type	TCP	UDP
Channel	Wireless	Wireless
Network Size	1000m X 1000m (x X y)	1000m X 1000m (x X y)
Routing Protocol	AODV	AODV
Number of nodes	50-300	50 to 300
Simulation time	200 seconds	200 seconds

Table 4.6 Performance of dynamically changing data rate

No. of nodes	Throughput (Kbps)		Packet Delivery Ratio (%)		Average End to End Delay (milliseconds)	
	TCP/ FTP	UDP/ CBR	TCP/ FTP	UDP/ CBR	TCP/ FTP	UDP/ CBR
50	476	46	97	99	500	90
100	580	90	97	98	646	190
150	445	130	95	94	913	240
200	472	157	92	90	950	385
250	380	166	84	88	1116	1140
300	691	140	78	80	2620	2330

4.7.1 Throughput

Figures 4.4and 4.5 show the simulation results of throughput while varying the number of offered loads for 100 nodes. In order to provide better performance of the network the system throughput must be high. The Figures 4.4 and 4.5 show the performance comparison of the existing High throughput Code aware Routing algorithm(HCOR) and the proposed ACAR routing algorithm based on transmission rate for random topology and grid topology for 100 nodes.

It is analyzed from the Figure 4.4 and figure 4.5 , the throughput of the proposed ACAR is gradually increasing compared to the existing high throughput code aware routing algorithm. In the proposed ACAR, the best coding opportunity paths are selected using optimal encoder algorithm based on anypath cost and delay. Therefore, the proposed ACAR gives better throughput using network coding in wireless mesh networks.

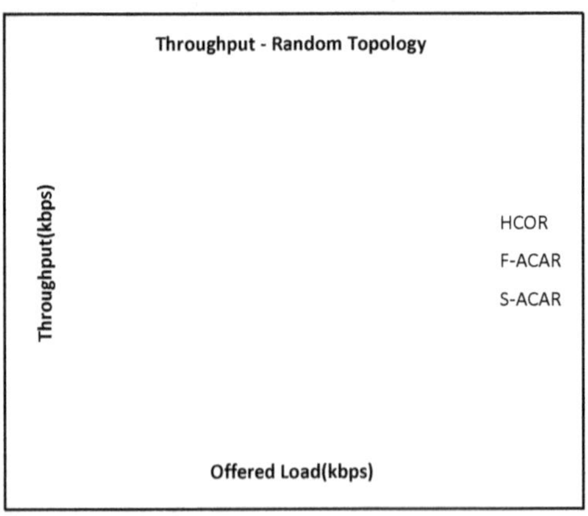

Figure 4.4 Throughput of ACAR and HCOR for random topology

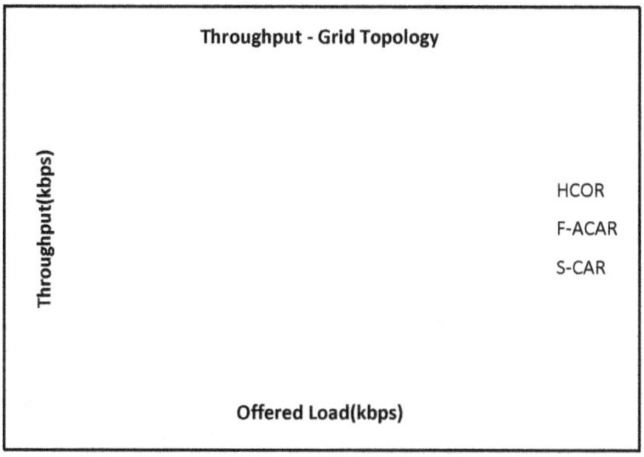

Figure 4.5 Throughput of ACAR and HCOR for grid topology

End-to-End delay

The end-to-end delay should be low in order to provide better performance. The Figures 4.6 and 4.7 show the performance graphs of routing end-to-end delay in continuous traffic pattern for HCOR and ACAR routing algorithms for random and grid topologies for 100 nodes.

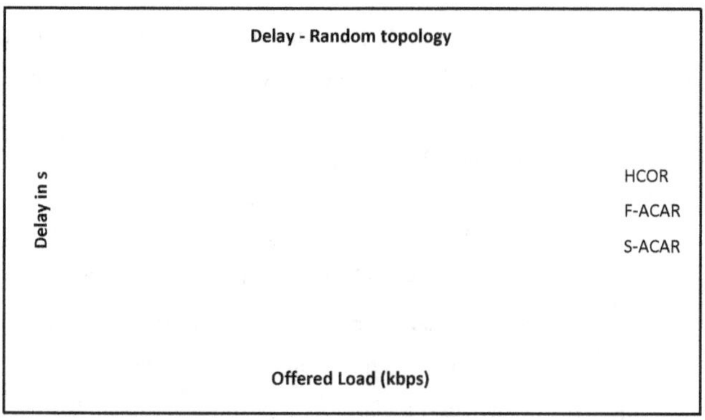

Figure 4.6 End-to-End delay of ACAR and HCOR for random topology

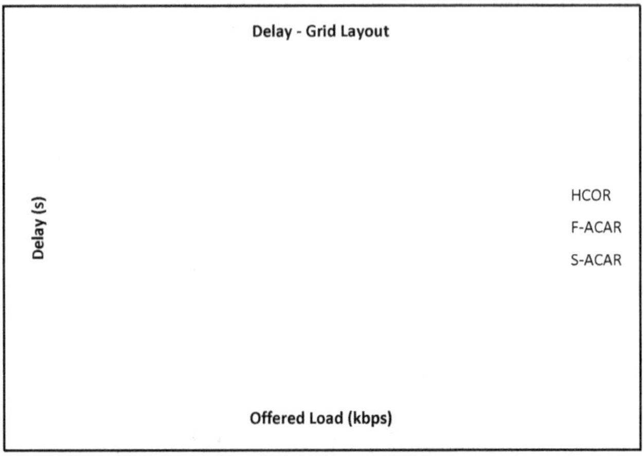

Figure 4.7 End-to-end delay of ACAR and HCOR for grid topology

In this proposed ACAR, due to the optimal encoder selection algorithm, best encoder node is selected among all the possible encoding nodes with two hop region based on the route metrics i.e anypath cost, delay and bandwidth. Based on the factors, ACAR selects the best routing path from the source to the destination and because of that, the packet can be delivered within time while increasing the speed. Thus, the proposed ACAR performs better with low end-to-end delay compared to the existing HCOR routing algorithms

Packet Delivery Ratio

The performance graphs in Figures 4.8 and 4.9 represent the packet delivery ratio of the existing HCOR algorithm and the proposed ACAR algorithm with respect to load for random and grid topologies for 100 nodes. Due to the optimal path selection using anypath cost, the best coding opportunities paths have been selected by the proposed ACAR. Thus, there is the possibility to receive more packets without any loss. Moreover, the proposed ACAR algorithm achieves high packet delivery ratio than the existing HOR algorithm and it gives better result.

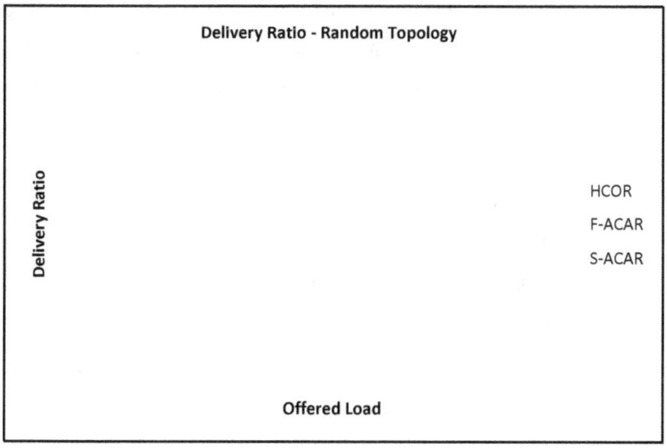

Figure 4.8 Packet Delivery ratio of ACAR and HCOR for random topology

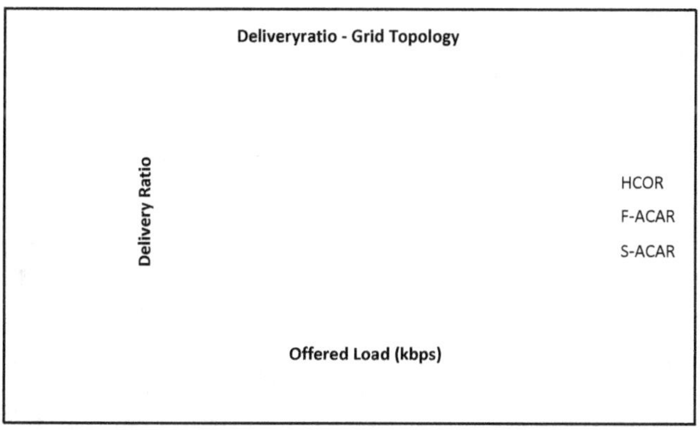

Figure 4.9 Packet Delivery of ACAR and HCOR for grid topology

SUMMARY

An Adaptive Coding Aware Routing Algorithm (ACAR), which is optimal encoding node selection algorithm has been proposed in network coding for wireless mesh networks. This routing algorithm incorporates potential coding opportunities into route selection using the 'Optimal Encoder Selection algorithm'. ACAR also adopts a more generalized coding scheme by eliminating the "two-hop" limitation in COPE [16]. By taking the advantage of Optimal Encoder Selection Algorithm, a computing method has been offered to calculate network coding cost, bandwidth estimation and delay in opportunistic transmission. The ACAR scheme has been implemented in NS-2 and extensive simulations are carried out. The simulation reveals substantial throughput gain over HCOR.

CHAPTERS

NETWORK CODING AWARE ROUTING ALGORITHM FOR THE ENHANCEMENT OF NETWORK PERFORMANCE IN WIRELESS MESH NETWORK (NET-CART)

This chapter presents a network coding aware routing algorithm (Net-CART) to avail the whole goodness of network-coding technique to increase the quantity of coding-opportunities in wireless mesh networks. To be safe from the packet loss, the incorrect packet encodings can be avoided and large number of packet encodings can be supported. It is essential to guarantee that the 'coding strategies' employed are necessary and correct. To override these difficulties, an improved set of coding strategies has been developed to identify large number of 'coding structures', to support more 'packet encodings'. Further, the novel routing algorithm has been designed to discover the path with more benefits riding on current network traffic patterns by utilizing the proposed coding conditions.

OVERVIEW

Network-coding combines all the packets based on the coding strategies to save the bandwidth. It should be noted that the packets are combined only if the coding strategies are satisfied. Also, to achieve the whole goodness of network-coding technique, it is important to increase the quantity of coding-opportunities. An improved set of coding strategies called Enhanced Universal Coding Strategies (EUCS) has been proposed to identify the large number of 'coding structures' and to support more 'packet encodings'. EUCS is also used to guide the structure of a novel WMNs routing algorithm referred to as Network Coding Aware Routing algorithm (Net-CART). A new routing-metric Code-Aware and Load-Aware Routing Metric (CALARM) has been proposed and that considers both the 'network workload' and 'coding-opportunities'. An improved set of coding strategies have been developed to identify all the possible coding-opportunities. However, the possible coding-opportunities are identified while promising that the native-packets embedded in the 'encoded' packets can be recovered successfully by their desired destinations.

A new WMNs routing algorithm is presented to monitor the route discovery process. This newly developed routing algorithm permits nodes to collect the essential details during route discoveries to evaluate whether it is possible to encode packets collectively depending on the newly developed coding strategies. The new routing-metric is established to combine both the 'code-aware' part and 'load-aware' part to support the source nodes in choosing the most ideal paths for packet transmission. Also, a mechanism is introduced for regular updating of this routing-metric.

The proposed Net-CART algorithm comprises an improved set of coding strategies and a new routing-metric and that considers both the coding-opportunities and network workload.

NETWORK-CODING AND CODING STRATEGIES

Ni *et al.* (2006) have examined the issues faced while changing the flows to generate numerous coding-opportunities, especially at the time of creating routing decisions. More significantly, they have developed the code awareness based ideal routing as same as that of a linear programming problem. Sengupta *et al.* (2007) have developed the hypothetical framework for 'coding aware routing'. This routing protocol evaluates the ideal paths by providing attention to all the routing requests and also has generated an attempt to increase the total network throughput. However, a linear programming model has been adapted by these centralized coding aware techniques to control the traffic, to distribute and to gather the topology. Also, these centralized routing approaches are operated based on centralized controller, which is hard to execute and to resolve the scalability issues in 'real-world' exploitation. More commonly, in wired networks, the data transmission occurs through 'multicast' flows and at this situation, to conserve the bandwidth, the network-coding concept has been introduced. Followed by this, in wireless mesh networks, the network-coding is introduced, due to its effectiveness in the preservation of bandwidth and it operates basically by adapting the notion of conventional COPE (S. Katti et. al,2008). This COPE mechanism inserts a coding among the two layers, such as, IP and MAC layers to improve the forwarding layer. Also, the network when trying to guarantee 'backward compatibility' with the conventional routing protocols, the COPE mechanism at the same time improves the network throughput. But, it should be noted that the network-coding in COPE mechanism functions perfectly only with two hops and hence, it minimizes the network performance. Further, this is considered as the major inadequacy faced by the COPE mechanism and limiting the performance gain. In COPE, to send

m different packets such as, $P_1, P_2, \ldots, P_m$ to m number of different next hops

$h_1, h_2, \ldots h_m$, in this a node is responsible to provide guarantee that all $m-1$ packets p_k are handled by each next hop h_j for all $k \neq j$. More importantly, the packet can be decoded completely through every next hop of an 'encoded' packet

according to this coding strategy. But, this is limited to only two-hops (i.e. it restricts the coding structure only to two-hops) and it should be noted that the coding-structure refers to the combination of flows/packets and encoding the combined packets collectively in a 'single' packet. Moreover, the encoding process occurs at the coding node. Also, the goodness of network-coding cannot be utilized completely and this leads to the notion of "coding-aware" routing. The idea of "coding-aware" routing is depicted well in Figure 5.1.

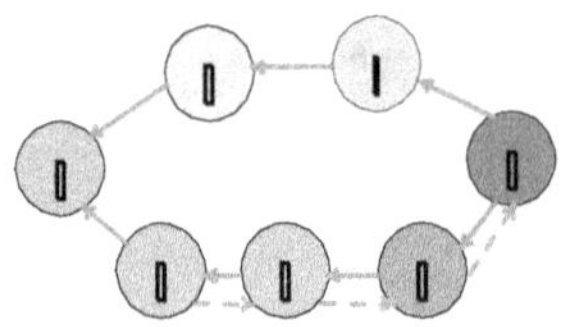

Figure S.1 Example for path selection with coding aware routing

The path from node 4 to node 3 (i.e. 4→5→6→3) is considered and the node-3 is willing to transmit its packets to node-2 through the existing flow. In case, after employing the hop-count metric, the route/path (i.e. 3→1→0→2) is selected by the node-3 over the route/path (i.e. 3→6→5→4→2) because of its minimum hop-count. However, coding is not performed well with this selection. Alternatively, at nodes 5 and 6, the packets can be encoded successfully by selecting the route/path 3→6→5→4→2, instead of 3→1→0→2. The two inadequacies faced by the "COPE" mechanism can be resolved with the Distributed Coding Aware Routing (DCAR) approach proposed by Le *et al.* (2010). The two inadequacies of "COPE" are as follows: a) only for about two-hops, the coding-structures are allowed (i.e. it is restricted to within a region of two-hops) b) coding-unaware routing. Therefore, the initial restriction inadequacy is resolved by establishing a set of coding strategies. However, the packets gained from two flows f_{e_1} and f_{e_2} meeting at node S can be encoded effectively only if the following strategies are satisfied.

a. For $D_1 \in d(S, f, \mathbf{e}_1)$ such that $D_1 \in n(S_2), S_2 \in u(S, f, \mathbf{e}_2)$, or $D_2 \in u(S, f, \mathbf{e}_1)$.

b. For $D_2 \in d(S, f, \mathbf{e}_2)$ such that $D_2 \in n(S_1), S_1 \in u(S, f, \mathbf{e}_1)$, or $D_2 \in u(S, f, \mathbf{e}_1)$.

Where the upstream, downstream, and the neighbor operators are denoted as $u(.)$, $d(.)$, and $n(.)$. In fact, to decode the packet completely, if the next hop that corresponds to an 'encoded' packet is not demanded or required, then the network-coding can occur by exceeding two-hops. The network illustrated in Figure 5.2 shows that for the encoded packets (P_1 EB P_2) the nodes 3 and 7 are identified as its next hops. However, the node 7 forwards the encoded packet (P_1 EB P_2), to node 8 and this occurs because, node 7 loses its ability to decode the encoded packets (P_1 EB P_2). Therefore, the node 7 uses the packet P_1 which is eavesdropped from node 1 and decodes the encoded packet (P_1 EB P_2) to recover the packet P_2. Then, the packet P_2 is forwarded to node 12 by the node 8. Thus, it is observed that DCAR is so much effective in overriding the two hop coding inadequacies in COPE. But, Guo B et.al (2011) have stated that the phenomenon referred to as 'false coding effect' is experienced by the coding strategies in DCAR. In order to eliminate this phenomenon, the coding strategies in DCAR are improved by adding numerous constraints. As a result, a novel set of coding strategies\conditions has been created and this is named as Generalized Coding Conditions(GCC). The coding strategies established in DCAR lead to the phenomenon 'false coding effect', due to few mis-interruptions of the coding strategies. The coding strategies in DCAR avoids the 'decoding' failures but they still experience an open issue in the improvement of coding strategies.

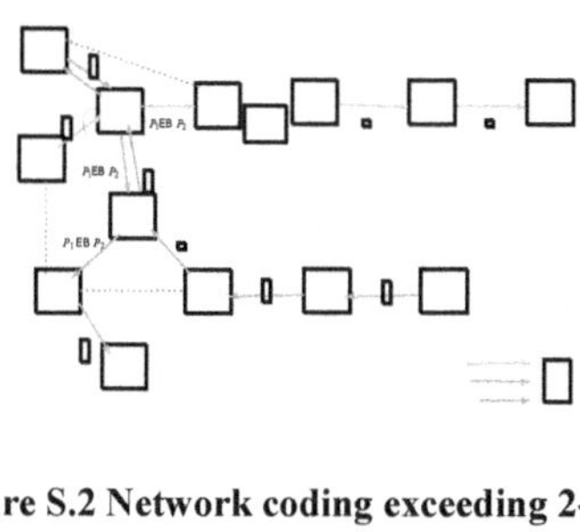

Figure S.2 Network coding exceeding 2-hops

The limitations of the GCC are as follows: Initially, it determines whether the packets can be encoded collectively based only on two cases. The initial case states that, only native-packets are encoded collectively. The next case states that all the packets are native-packets and among these native-packets, only one will be an 'encoded' packet. If more than two packets are allowed to encode collectively, then these two cases fail to show its potentiality in encoding the packets and this may lead to the loss of few coding-opportunities. The second issue relays on determining whether an encoded packet is possible to be encoded again with the native-packet based on 'onion peeling like approach' employed in GCC. The problem inferred in this method is explained in the Figure 5.3. The superficial (potential) coding node determines whether the superficially encoded packet can be decoded completely, if the following is true: a) node 1 uses the eavesdropped (overheard) coding flows $f_{,e_1}$ EB $f_{,e_3}$ to decode the encoded packet. After this, the partially decoded packet is forwarded to node 2, b) the received packet cannot be decoded by the node 2 and this packet is forwarded to node-3and c) node 3 uses the eavesdropped (overheard) native flows $f_{,e_1}$ and $f_{,e_4}$ to decode the received packet. The 'onion peeling like approach states that the packets are allowed to be 'encoded' collectively only at the situation that the decoding sequence still remains alive to permit the resultant 'encoded' packet to be decoded completely and immediately the packet reaches the destination of the corresponding native-flow. However, the packet encoding done by means of decoding sequence is not supported with the 'downstream' nodes that are meant to the coding node and hence, it results in decoding failure.

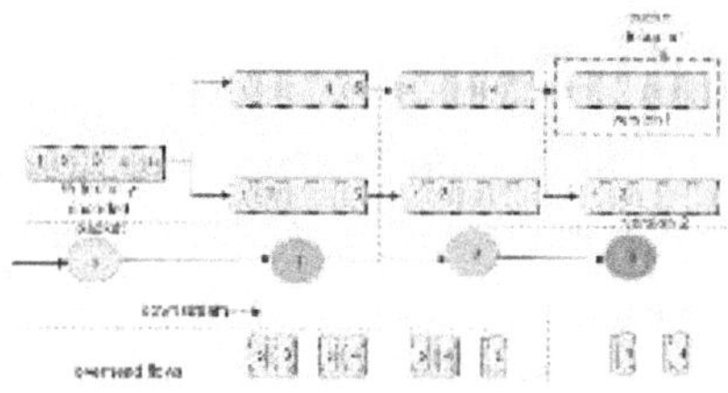

Figure S.3 Encoding and decoding packets using "onion-peeling-like"

S.2.1 Route Metrics

The route metric is commonly employed in the networks to make the routing decisions. It is a measure used to rank paths based on some conditions. Most of the conventional routing protocols adopt the hop-count routing metric and these routing metric fail to consider the coding-opportunities, Hence, it loses its ability to realize the full advantage of network-coding.

The Coding Aware Multi path (CAMP) routing protocol (Han *et al.* 2008) uses the commonly known Expected Transmission Count Metrics (ETX) (De Couto *et al.* ,2003). A source node in the CAMP after identifying the coding gain moves dynamically from one path to the next path. However, the packets available in the path can be finely encoded with the extra packets, but they fail to consider this advantage. While employing the network coding for successful transmission of packets between the nodes, it is essential to compute the expected number of transmission needed for successful transfer (exchange) of packets. Therefore, to accomplish this criteria, the Expected number of coded transmissions for an Exchange (ECX) (Ni *et al.* 2006 & Zhang *et al.* 2017) routing metric is used. This metric allows the retransmission to improve the network from the packets loss. It should be noted that this ECX routing metric has been specifically designed based on two hop coding-structure and due to this fact, it fails to cooperate well with the general network-coding criterions which can occur beyond two-hops. In order to transmit the newly incoming packet and the existing packets successfully to the next hop, the Coding Aware Routing Metric(CRM) employed in the DCAR routing protocol is used to evaluate the expected number of transmissions required for successful transmission of packets. The main issue faced with CRM approach is that it unnecessarily takes into account the already used packets remaining in the considered path or on the 'network interface queues' of the nodes. But during this process, it forgets to update the routing-metric value of the considerable path. The Multi-Rate Algorithm (MRA) (Vieira *et al.* 2013), transmits the packets without considering the path conditions and capacity such as contention, interference and bandwidth etc. Moreover, the Multi-path Routing Throughput (MRT) approach (Qureshi *et al.* 2014) exploits the attainable bandwidth of the transmitting paths in the presence of neighboring interferences and link error. In order to compute the existence of coding-opportunities in considerable path, the Free-ride Oriented Routing Metric(FORM) (Guo *et al.* 2011) is designed with two parts such as, i) B_M (Modified Benefit) and ii) Deg_{fr} (degree of free-ride). To transmit a packet on the 'considered-path', the B_M computes the difference between the hop-count increase and hop-count decrease and sends the packets through the considered path rather than transmitting the packets to the shortest path. Whereas, the overflow of coding -opportunities in the considered path is computed using Deg_{fr}. The path with maximum FORM value is selected as the best path for packet transmission. Additionally, the inadequacy faced with FORM is that it can determine the FORM values of paths only during route discoveries and it forgets the regular updating.

Net-CART solution is proposed to improve the coding-opportunities beyond two hops. The Net-CART protocol follows the route discovery process of DSR approach; because it provides complete information about the path before sending its packets to its corresponding destination. Also, none of the above mentioned works has aimed on the elimination of incorrect packet encodings and therefore, it is essential to construct an effective routing metric and routing strategy to improve the throughput performance of the network.

GENERAL CODING CONDITIONS

More importantly, following the basics of Dynamic Source Routing (DSR) protocol (Blywis *et al.* 2010), the Net-CART has been proposed for perfect transmission of packets to the destination. The main notion behind adapting the basics of DSR protocol for the development of Net-CART protocol is due to the fact that the source routing of DSR allows gathering complete knowledge about the path prior to sending a packet by its source. Thus, beyond two hops, it allows the *network coding* and *coding aware routing.* In order to perform the coding aware routing, it is essential to follow the coding aware routing metric for the selection of optimal or best path by a source node. More significantly, after the selection of best path by a source node, it sends the packet to the destination. However, to perform the destination vector routing, if the Ad-hoc On-Demand Distance Vector (AODV) routing protocol (Perkins & Royer 1999) is selected, then there might be an experience of collision in the transmission of packets through the optimal path (i.e. packets may not traverse on the optimal end to end path). This inadequacy occurs because, source node in AODV routing protocol obtains the ability to evaluate alone the next hop alone and fails to determine the entire path that a packet could reach to its destination. However, in 'source' routing, the packet headers record the details about the entire path and this in turn allows more superior 'coding nodes' to take decisions whether it is possible to encode the packets further than the (beyond) two hops (Yang & Yang 2010, Wunderlich *et al.* 2017, Qin *et al.* 2016). Conversely, with the destination vector routing, the coding-opportunities are neglected, due to the fact that this superior coding-node involves detecting only the next subsequent hops of a packets which are encoded potentially. Also, this superior coding node tries to identify only the destinations of the native-packets that correspond to the superior encoded packets. For instance, assume the network in Figure 5.3. In node 2, the packets from the flows f_{e_1} and f_{e_2} are encoded collectively. Conversely, when the AODV routing protocol is applied, the node-2 can't identify the neighboring downstream nodes in the flows (i.e. node-2 can't identify that node 8 is one of its downstream nodes in flow f_{e_2}). This situation arises because node-2 possesses the ability to find only its next hop in the flow f_{e_2} and node-12 which means its corresponding destination. Therefore, a coding opportunity is neglected, due to the fact that node-2 fails to encode both P_1 and P_2, collectively.

Coding Strategies

An improved set of coding strategies called Enhanced Universal Coding Strategies (EUCS) is also proposed to determine large number of coding-opportunities. It should be noted that the coding opportunities may be neglected with stricter coding strategies. For instance, only for about two hops, the coding structures are limited in COPE. In Net-CART, more numbers of anticipated receivers receive an encoded packet which is broadcasted through coding node. Hence, the pseudo broadcasting condition is followed by the coding node. However, this pseudo broadcasting condition is much similar to the network coding approaches such as, FORM (Guo *et al.* 2011) , DCAR (Le *et al.* 2010) and COPE (Katti *et al.* 2008). The procedures of pseudo broadcast are as follows: Instead of considering the address of next hop that is attached on the packet, the pseudo broadcast considers the addresses of other anticipated receivers to unicast a packet to next hop. Hence, this anticipated receiver is named as 'pseudo broadcast receiver'. The received packet is merged onto the enqueued packet at the time of encoding (combining) two packets. Some of the terms, which are used to define the EUCS, are illustrated in Table 5.1.

Table S.1 Terms used in EUCS

Terms	Description
$f{,}e^{*}_{r}$	The initial (primary) flow of the received packet
$f{,}e^{*}_{q}$	The initial (primary) flow of the enqueued packet
$f{,}e_{r}$	The native-packet flow in the received packet
$f{,}e_{q}$	The native-packet flow in the enqueued packet
$F{,}e_{r}$	All native-packet flows (set of flows) in the received packet
$F{,}e_{q}$	All native-packet flows (set of flows) in the enqueued packet
Next-hop $(y, f{,}e)$	The next hop of node y in flow $f{,}e$
$d(y, f{,}e)$	All downstream nodes (i.e. set of downstream nodes) of node y in flow $f{,}e$
$u(y, f{,}e)$	All upstream nodes (i.e. set of upstream nodes) of node y in flow fw
$u_{native}(y, f{,}e)$	All upstream nodes that corresponds to node y in flow $f{,}e$; where a native-packet of flow $f{,}e$ is transmitted natively
$n(y)$	The set of neighbors of node y
P_r	A pseudo broadcast receiver that corresponds to the enqueued packet
I. P_r	Set of all pseudo broadcast receivers that corresponds to the enqueued packet
fl_{P_r}	The initial (primary) flow of the pseudo broadcast receiver P_r. It represents the primary flow obtained at the time an encoded packet reached to P_r.

The EUCS is normally stated as follows: More importantly, before encoding two packets (i.e. each of the packets can be either native or encoded) collectively, a superior (potential) coding node S should satisfy the following criterions and they are illustrated below in Table 5.2.

Table S.2 Coding Strategies

Sl. No	Strategies
1	next-hop $(S, f{,}e^{*}_{r})$ -: next-hop $(S, f{,}e^{*}_{q})$

2	next-hop $(S, f.e^{\bullet}_r)$ -: P_r , 'v' P_r E |. P_r
3	$3N_1$ E $d(S, f.e^{\bullet}_q)$ U $(n(d(S, f.e^{\bullet}_q)) \setminus \{S\})$ such that N_1 E $u_{native}(S, f.e_r)$'v' $f.e_r$ E $F.e_r$.
4	$3N_2$ E $d(S, f.e_{P_r})$ U $(n(d(S, f.e))_{P_r} \setminus \{S\})$ such that N_2 E $u_{native}(S, f.e_r)$'v' $f.e_r$ E $F.e_r$, 'v' P_r E |. P_r .
5	$3N_3$ E $d(S, f.e^{\bullet}_r)$ U $(n(d(S, f.e^{\bullet}_r)) \setminus \{S\})$ such that N_3 E $u_{native}(S, f.e_q)$'v' $f.e_q$ E $F.e_q$.

Strategies I and 2: This illustrates that the next hop of node S located in the initial (primary) flow that corresponds to the 'received packet' should not be equal to the next hop of node S located in the initial (primary) flow and that relates to the 'enqueued packet' not to some of the pseudo broadcast receivers that corresponds to the 'enqueued packet'. Moreover, these two strategies guarantee that the anticipated (intended) receivers are same for entire resultant 'encoded' packet.

Strategy 3: It states that, in the initial (primary) flow of the 'enqueued' packet, there comprises a set of 'downstream' nodes related to S and there exists a condition that there should be the presence of node in the 'downstream' nodes related to S for each and every native-flow in the 'received' packet. This strategy guarantees that the encoded packet before reaching the destination of the initial (primary) flow of the 'enqueued' packet or else on the received time itself, the resultant 'encoded' packet can be decoded completely.

Strategy 4: There exists a set of possible native-flow combinations in the received packet and the 'enqueued packet includes the pseudo broadcast receiver. Whereas, for both these facts, a condition exists that, there should be the presence of node in the set of 'downstream' nodes related to S in the initial (primary) flow of the 'pseudo broadcast' receiver. Also, their neighbors are considered as an 'upstream' node of s in the native-flow of the 'received' packet. This strategy guarantees that the encoded packet before reaching the destination of the initial (primary) flow of the 'pseudo broadcast' receivers or else on the received time itself, the resultant 'encoded' packet can be decoded completely.

***Strategy** 5:* The enqueued packet comprises set of native-flows and for each native-flow, there exists a condition that there should be the presence of node in the set of downstream nodes related to s in the initial (primary) flow of the received packet. Furthermore, their neighbors are also considered as an upstream node of s in the native-flow of the enqueued packet. This strategy guarantees that the encoded packet before reaching the destination of the initial (primary) flow of the received packet or else on the received time itself, the resultant encoded packet can be decoded completely.

The strategies 3 and 4 determine whether the enqueued packet can hold the received packet or not and the strategy 5 determines whether the received packet can hold the enqueued packet or not. More significantly, the strategies 3 to 5 collectively ensure that the destinations of the native-packets can recover their corresponding native-packets embedded in the resultant encoded packet (i.e. native-packets in the resultant encoded' packets can be recovered by their respective destinations). Thus, two or more packets can be encoded collectively in an effective way.

For example, the network shown in Figure 5.4 includes 3 coding models such as, i) a native-packet that belongs to flow $f_{,\mathbf{e}_1}$ (i.e. P_1 with a native-packet of flow $f_{,\mathbf{e}_2}$, which means P_2 is at node 1 (n_1)); ii) a native-packet that belongs to flow $f_{,\mathbf{e}_1}$ (i.e. P_1 with a native-packet of flow $f_{,\mathbf{e}_3}$, which means P_3 is at node 2) and iii) an 'encoded' packet that belongs to flows $f_{,e_1}$ EB $f_{,e_2}$ (i.e.

encoding the packets P_1 EB P_2 at n_1 by considering the native-packet of flow f,e $_3$, which means the packet P_3 is at n_2 (node 2)). The initial two cases exhibit trivial solution and therefore, it is demonstrated how EUCS performs well on the third case for 'packet' encoding. Let us consider the 'enqueued' packet as P_3 and received packet as $P_1 \mathrm{EB} P_2$, respectively. The values assumed to the above explained terms are as follows:

- S=2

- $f_r e_r^* = f_r e_{r_1} = f_r e_1 = 0 \rightarrow 1 \rightarrow 2 \rightarrow 6$

■ $f, \mathbf{e}_r^{\bullet} = f, \mathbf{e}_{r_1} = f, \mathbf{e}_1 = 0 \rightarrow 1 \rightarrow 2 \rightarrow 6$

- $f_e r_2 = f_e 2 = 5 \rightarrow 3 \rightarrow 1 \rightarrow 4$

- $F_e r = \{ f_e r_1, f_e r_2 \}$

■ $f,\mathbf{e}_q^{\bullet} = f,\mathbf{e}_{q_1} = f,\mathbf{e}_3 = 6 \rightarrow 2 \rightarrow 1$

- F ,e $_q$ = {f,e $_{q_1}$}

- |. P_r = �

- *Next-hop (S=2, f,e,*˙*)=6*

- *Next-hop* $(S{=}2,\ f,\mathbf{e}_q^{*})=I$

- $d(S=2, f, \mathbf{e}_q^{\cdot}) = \{I\}$
- $n(d(S=2, f, \mathbf{e}_q^{\cdot})) \backslash \{2\} = n(I) \backslash \{2\} = \{0,2,3,4\} \backslash \{2\} = \{0,3,4\}$

- $d(S=2,\ f,\mathbf{e}_q^{\bullet}) \cup (n(d(S=2,\ f,\mathbf{e}^{\bullet}))\setminus\{2\})=\{I\} \cup \{0,3,4\}=\{0,I,3,4\}$

q

- $u(S=2, f, \mathbf{e}_{r1}) = \{0,1\}$
- $u_{native}(S=2, f, \mathbf{e}_{r1}) = \{0\}$

- $u_{native}(S=2, f, \mathbf{e}_{r_2}) = \{3,5\}$
- $d(S=2, f, \mathbf{e}_r^*) = \{6\}$
- $n(d(S=2, f, \mathbf{e}_q^*)) \setminus \{2\} = n(I) \setminus \{2\} = \{0,2,3,4\} \setminus \{2\} = \{0,3,4\}$

- $d(S=2,\ f, \mathbf{e}_q^{\bullet}) \cup (n(d(S=2,\ f, \mathbf{e}^{\bullet})) \setminus \{2\}) = \{1\} \cup \{0,3,4\} = \{0,1,3,4\}$

q

- $u(S=2, f, \mathbf{e}_{r_1}) = \{0,1\}$
- $u_{native}(S=2, f, \mathbf{e}_{r_1}) = \{0\}$
- $u_{native}(S=2, f, \mathbf{e}_{r_2}) = \{3,5\}$
- $d(S=2, f, \mathbf{e}^{*}_{r}) = \{6\}$
- $n(d(S=2, f, \mathbf{e}^{*}_{r})) \setminus \{2\} = n\{6\} \setminus \{2\} = \{2,5\} \setminus \{2\} = \{5\}$
- $d(S=2, f, \mathbf{e}^{*}_{r}) \cup (n(d(S=2, f, \mathbf{e}^{*}_{r})) \setminus \{2\}) = \{6\} \cup \{5\} = \{5,6\}$

- $u(S=2,\ f.\mathbf{e}_{r1}) = \{6\}$

- $u_{native}(S=2, f_{,e_{q1}}) = \{6\}$

Whereas, Next-hop (S=2, $f_{,e_r^*}$) = 6 is not equal to Next-hop (S=2, $f_{,e_q^*}$) = 1. Hence, it satisfies the strategy 1. It should be noted that it is not so much important to verify the strategy 2, due to the fact that $|.P_r = \phi$. The term $u_{native}(S, f_{,e})$ is demanded by the strategies 3 to 5 and this can be obtained from the stored information in packets (i.e. at which nodes the native-packets in them are transmitted natively). For instance, before encoding two packets collectively at n_1 (node 1), the packet P_2 is passed (transmitted) natively on the nodes 3 and 5. Hence, without encoding any other packet P_1 is passed (transmitted) 'natively' at node 0. Moreover, $u_{native}(S=2, f, \mathbf{e}_{r_1}) = \{0\}$ and $u_{native}(S=2\, f, \mathbf{e}_{r_2}) = \{3,5\}$ are included.

While $0 \in d(S=2, f, e^{*}) \cup (n(d(S=2, f, e^{*}))\backslash\{2\})$ and $0 \in u_{native}(S=2, f, e)$ and $3 \in d(S=2,$

q *q* r_1

$f,e^{\cdot}$) ∪ (n(d(S=2, $f,e^{\cdot}$))\{2}) and 3 ∈ u_{native}(S=2, f,e) ,the strategy 3 is satisfied. It is not

q q $r2$

so much essential to verify the strategy 4, due to the fact that $|.\ P_r = ◆$. The strategy 5 is satisfied with $6 \in d(S{=}2,\ f_r e^{\cdot}) \cup (n(d(S{=}2,\ f_r e^{\cdot}))\setminus\{2\})$ and $6 \in u_{native}(S{=}2\ f_r e_{q_1})$. It is not so much essential to verify the strategy 4, due to the fact that $|.\ P_r = ◆$. The

r r

strategy 5 is satisfied with $6 \in d(S=2, f,e^{\cdot}) \cup (n(d(S=2, f,e^{\cdot}))\setminus\{2\})$ and $6 \in$

u_{native}(S=2 *f*,e q_1) . The packets are encoded collectively where all the strategies of EUCS are satisfied effectively. The resultant encoded packets obtained after encoding two packets have the following conditions such as next hop=1,

t_{P_r} r 1

l. $P_r = \{6\}$, and $= 6 = f_r \mathbf{e}^* = f_r \mathbf{e}_r = f_r \mathbf{e}_1 = 0 \rightarrow 1 \rightarrow 2 \rightarrow 6$. Altogether, the next hop that corresponds to the resultant encoded packet (i.e. node 1) and the single pseudo broadcast receiver of the resultant encoded packet (i.e. node 6) combines to generate the set of anticipated receivers that belong to the resultant encoded packet. In the above illustrated example, initially at node 2, the packets P_3 and P_1 EB P_2 are encoded collectively. Then, for the 'enqueued' packet P_3, it follows I. P_r = ◆ and hence, the strategies 3 and 4 are not verified. These strategies are applied only if the packets are 'encoded' collectively numerous (multiple) times at a node.

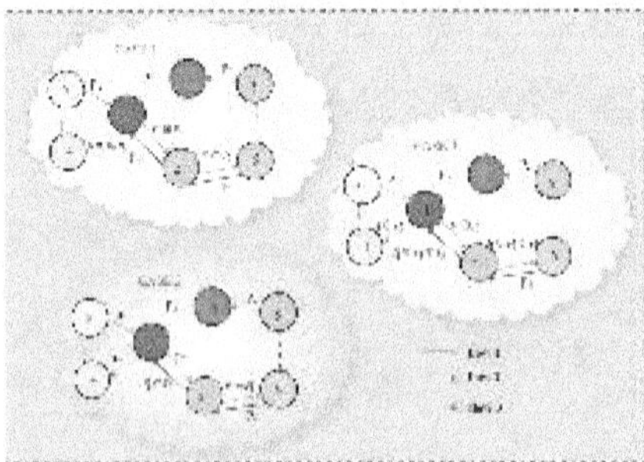

Figure S.4 The illustrative-network

For instance, consider the packets such as P_1, P_2 and P_3 are to be encoded collectively at a node. Then, the two packets P_1 and P_2 are encoded for the first time and for the encoded packets (i.e. P_1 EB P_2), I. P_r turns to be a non-empty set which means I. P_r = ◆ . Also, to compute the encoded packets P_1 EB P_2, the strategies 4 and 5 are employed and the obtained resultant packet is then encoded with the packet P_3.

Route Discovery

A node in the Net-CART approach adapts the EUCS to find whether the packets can be encoded collectively or not. In order to allow a node to collect its essential information, the route-discovery process of the DSR (Blywis *et al.* 2010) is improved. The steps are explained as follows:

Step 1: *Initiating an improved route-discovery process:* At the packets destination, if there experiences a lack of valid route and a node at the time wishes to transmit a packet to their respective destination, then it leads to multipath traffic/congestion. Therefore, to withstand this issue, a node transmits a *route request* referred to as 'RREQ' to initiate a new route discovery process.

Step 2: *Managing the received route request:* After receiving a route request (RREQ) by a node, it tries to neglect the route looping through analyzing the route details (record) of RREQ. In case, the RREQ traverses through the node, then that particular RREQ is dropped. Also, the route request (RREQ) is dropped by a node by maintaining a broadcast ID cache of RREQs (i.e. the node drops the RREQs and it's not an original route request (duplicate copy)). The node that doesn't drop the route request (RREQ) is considered as the RREQ destination and then to the RREQ source, the node sends back the RREP (route reply). If the node fails to drop the RREQ and is not considered as the RREQ destination, at this situation, the node combines its address with the route details (records) of the RREQ. After this process, the node forwards the RREQ.

Step 3: *Replying route requests (RREQs):* The RREP (route reply) packet is generated by the RREQ destination immediately after receiving a route request (RREQ). Then, the value of RREP is set to 0 in the metric field. Subsquently, through the reversed path which is traverseed by the RREQ, it sends the route reply (RREP) to the RREQ source.

Step 4: *Managing the received route replys:* The node after receiving a route reply (RREP), it stores (records) their corresponding neighbors and its downstream nodes. After this process, if the node is recognized as an intermediate node, then it stores (records) its neighborhood information in the RREP. Followed by this, the metric-field that corresponds to RREP is updated prior to the transmission of RREP to the next hop. On the other hand, the metric-field of the RREP is updated after determining the node as the RREQ source. Then, the updated value in the metric-field of RREP is recorded in the routing table along with the route (path) that is associated to the RREP.

As compared to FORM, Net-CART uses minimum number of RREQs to generate routing and coding decisions (i.e. information needed to generate routing and the coding decisions are not propagated using RREQs). More importantly, the transmission time required by the largest packets is more and the network performance is highly degraded with large RREQs. This inadequacy occurs because of the duplication of RREQs and these duplicated RREQs are transmitted throughout the whole network by adapting the route discovery process. Alternatively, in Net-CART, the information needed to generate routing and the coding decisions are broadcasted using RREPs. Unlike RREQs, the RREPs are traversed only through certain nodes instead of transmitting them through the whole network. Furthermore, the RREPs in FORM are larger than the number of RREPs in Net-CART because, the FORM needs to carry more number of information than the Net-CART.

For instance, consider the network depicted in Figure 5.4. It illustrates the route discovery process employed by the Net-CART approach. The flow f_{e_1} considers the node 0 as its source. The flow f_{e_2} considers the node 5 as its source and the flow f_{e_3} considers the node 6 as its source. At first, the node 0 doesn't identify its route to node 6. Therefore, a node 0 tries to initiate a new route to node 6 by sending a route request (RREQ) (i.e. the node 0 initiates a new route discovery process). Assume that, the node 6 travels through the route (path) 0, 1, 2, and 6 (i.e. $0 \rightarrow 1 \rightarrow 2 \rightarrow 6$). A new route reply (RREP) is generated by node 6 immediately after receiving the route request (RREQ). The value of RREP is then initialized in the metric-field as 0. The nodes 2 and 5 are the neighbor nodes of node 6 and the node 6 in turn stores (records) the addresses of its neighbor nodes onto RREP. Figure 5.5(a) depicts the current format of RREP. After this process, to the RREQ source, the node 6 transmits the RREP through the reversed route (path) which is traversed by the RREQ. The node 2 can observe the neighbors of node 6 after receiving the RREP from node 6. However, the node 2 is not considered as an RREP destination, and then the RREP is further improved by the node 2; which means, the node 2 observes the addresses of its nearest neighbor nodes 1 and 6 and the observed addresses are stored/recorded onto the packet. Also, the metric-field value is updated effectively in the packet. Figure 5.5(b) depicts the format of improved packet. Assume that, the metric-field value in the RREP is increased by one. It should be noted that, it is not possible to determine the updated metric-field value for the path $0 \rightarrow 1 \rightarrow 2 \rightarrow 6$ in accurate manner (i.e. when it is increased by one). This is due to the fact that, it depends wholly on the 'network queue-interface' utilization and the number of packets in the 'network queue-interface' of node 2. The packets associated with the 'network queue-interface' of node 2 can be 'encoded' collectively with the packet travelling through the path $0 \rightarrow 1 \rightarrow 2 \rightarrow 6$.

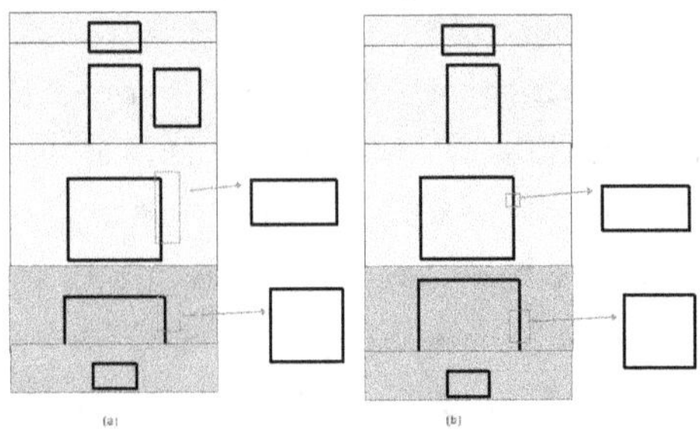

Figure S.S: Route Reply (RREP) contents at node-6 (a) and node-2 (b)

After this process, the node-2 forwards the packet. This process is continued till the RREP reaches its destination (i.e. node 0). This provides a way to identify the neighbors of the downstream nodes by the upstream nodes. On the other hand, it can be stated that the upstream nodes can observe their downstream nodes. According to Figure 5.4, in case 1, the node 1 is determined as a superficial coding-node for the flows f_{e_1} and f_{e_2}. For example, the route discovery process explained above has obtained the following knowledge for the node 1. They are as follows: a) its neighbors and the downstream nodes in flow f_{e_1}, b) its upstream nodes in flow f_{e_1}; c) its neighbors and downstream nodes in flow f_{e_2} and d) its upstream nodes in flow f_{e_2}. Moreover, with the help of EUCS, the node-1 can determine whether the packets employed in these two flows can be encoded collectively or not.

CALCULATIONS OF ROUTE METRICS

Code-Aware and Load-Aware Routing Metric (CALARM)

Beyond this newly developed coding strategies, it is essential to bulid a new route metric to utilize the whole goodness of network coding advantage to further enhance the network throughput. Before computing route metric, some of the quailities of an optimal path are required for packet transmission. i) Minimum transmision-count: The interference occurrence and the highly degraded channel contention can be minimized with the route experiencing minimum transmission-count. Also, by minimizing unwanted transmission in the network, the route can save bandwidth. ii) More coding-opportunities: The bandwidth is highly saved by the routes holding large number of coding-opportunities (i.e. the coding-opportunities allow the packets to be combined to save the bandwidth) and iii) Removing the congested nodes: For a busy node, the network interface queue could not be empty. In this case, the network experiences a packet loss because, a node is forced to drop the newly arrived packets.

More significantly, the packets are opportunistically encoded by the nodes and to encode them, the packets are not delayed during transmission. In this case, the nodes with fully filled 'network interface queues' can make the packet encoding process faster as possible. However, the packets, when transmitted through longer routes/paths, may cause interference and large amount of channel contention. Hence, these two limitations make the network interface queues of the nodes to be in filled state and therefore, it allows more coding-opportunities. On the other hand, it should be noted that even though after generating more number of packet encodings, the network throughput is not improved in such type of situation. Consequently, modelling a routing-metric is necessary to control the transmission count with increase in the number of coding-opportunities carefully. As a result, a routing-metric named as CALARM (Code-Aware and Load-Aware Routing Metric) has been proposed and it is modeled based on the condition: using small amount of transmission as well as considering the coding-opportunities to transmit a packet from source to its respective destination. The code-aware part and the load-aware part are combined together to form CALARM routing-metric.

Code-Aware Routing Metric

The term $1-P_{ENC_m}^{p_j}$ refers to the code-aware portion in which the considerable path is termed as p_j and a function that associates (maps) the sum of native-packets from other different paths p_j is denoted as $P_{ENCm}^{p_j}$. At node *m*, the packet from p_j can be encoded at the criterion $\forall k \neq j$, where $m \in p_j, m \neq dist(p_j)$

is used to measure the real limit [0,1]. The function P p_j can be computed

ENC_m

using Equation. (5.1).

$$P^{p_j} = (\quad \frac{1}{} X \quad 1.num- \quad p_k \tag{5.1}$$

$ENC_m \quad \min 1.0, \quad packets_m$

p_j encoded with $p_k, k \neq j$)

Consider the packet at node m and the packet in turn traverses through the path p_j. After this, the packet is referred as the considered-packet and the node is referred as the considered-node. The considered-node encodes the considered-packet and $P_{ENC_m}^{p_j}$ as the probability (confidence) for the encoded packet. The considered-node loses its ability to encode the considered-packet, if $P_{ENC_m}^{p_j} = 0$. Similar to this, if $P_{ENC_m}^{p_j} = 1$, then the considered-node can effectively encode the considered-packet. Also, $1 - P_{ENC_m}^{p_j}$ be the number of broadcasts (transmissions) required by the considered node to transmit the considered packet to the next hop. To transmit/route the considered-packet over the path holding, the nodes possessing more number of packets on their network interface queues and then, these packets can be finely encoded with the considered-packet. Alternatively, the considered-node possessing small number of packets on their network interface queue can also be encoded with the considered-packet. For example, in some criteria, the time at which one or two considered-packets reaching the considered-node can't be encoded appropriately with those packets, due to the fact that those packets remain alive for minimum period in a path (Yuan Chai et al, 2017).

To recover the hardness in obtaining $P_{ENC_m}^{p_j} = 0$, the threshold parameter μ is adjusted and set to 1, which means the maximum network interface queue length. In case, the threshold parameter is adjusted to 0, then this will make the $P_{ENC_m}^{p_j}$ and $1 - P_{ENC_m}^{p_j}$ to always consider the values between 1 and 0. Beyond this, the threshold parameter μ after setting to 0 in turn, changes every path to look similar with a CALARM value of'0'. It should be careful that the value provided for μ should not exceed the maximum network interface queue length and sometimes, if it exceeds the value, then the $P_{ENC_m}^{p_j}$ faces the difficulty in attaining the measure of 1.0. This shows that, network interface queue not assumes, how many considered nodes are involved to encode the considered packet. When a threshold parameter μ is set to a lowest value, then it is enough for the considered-node holding some packets in its network interface queues to be encoded with the considered-packet. Therefore, through this encoding process, $P_{ENC_m}^{p_j}$ obtains the value equal to '1.0'. On the reverse process, if a threshold parameter μ is set to a greater value, then it is enough for the considered-node holding more number of packets in its network interface queues to be encoded with the considered-packet. Therefore, through this encoding process, $P_{ENC_m}^{p_j}$ obtains the value equal to '1.0'. When a threshold parameter μ is set to a lowest value, then it turns to be a non-complex process for $P_{ENC_m}^{p_j}$ to acquire the value equal to '1.0'. Throughout the simulation process, the value of threshold parameter μ is set to 1.0 (i.e. which corresponds to 10% of 100) and this value is observed as the common measure used in the wireless network simulations to increase the network interface queue length.

Load Aware Routing Metric

The term $1/LS_m^{pj}$ represents the load aware portion of the CALARM approach, whereas, the function that associates (maps) with the network interface queue utilization (i.e. non-empty network interface queue in %) of node-*m* is referred to as LS_m^{pj}. The queue utilization value (i.e. queue-utilization$_m$) is set in the real limit of 0 to 1. Moreover, the load signal of the 'considered-node' m is viewed as $1/LS_m^{pj}$. This term is mainly used to prevent the source nodes activity from transmitting (sending) their packets on traffic path (i.e. the path with more number of congested nodes or the nodes with

m

maximum network interface 'queue' utilization). The function LS^{pj} is computed with Eqution (5.2).

$$LS^{pj} = \left(\frac{1}{\;} \times queue - utilization + \frac{1}{\;} \right. \quad (5.2)$$

161

m min 1.0, 11 -1.0 m 1.0 −11)

As mentioned above, $1\text{-}P_{ENC_m}^{pj}$ be the number of broadcasts (transmissions) required by the considered node to transmit the considered packet to the next hop. More importantly, the number of broadcasts (transmissions) required by the considered node to transmit the considered packet to the next hop is improved by multiplying the term γLS_m^{pj} with $1\text{-}P_{ENC_m}^{pj}$. Also, when compared to the threshold parameter 11, if the network interface 'queue' utilization of the considered-node exhibits equal or lesser value, then the function LS_m^{pj} equals to 1. At the situation, when LS_m^{pj} is equal to 1, then the term $1\text{-}P^{pj}$ is not improved (i.e. $(1\text{-}P^{pj})/1=1\text{-}P^{pj}$)). This states that the

ENC_m ENC_m ENC_m

number of broadcasts (transmissions) required by the considered node to transmit the considered packet to the next hop depends on the decision that the considered-node has the ability to encode the considered-packet or not. However, when compared to the threshold measure11 , if the network interface queue utilization, that corresponds to the considered-node, exhibits greater value, then the function LS_m^{Pj} considers the value in the real-limit [0, 1].

At this situation, the number of broadcasts (transmissions) required by the considered node to transmit the considered packet to the next hop is increased to a maximum value of $((1-P_{ENC_m}^{Pj})/LS_m^{Pj} > 1-P_{ENC_m}^{Pj})$. This is done to suppress the consideration of paths that involve the 'considered-node'. This paves the way to design LS_m^{Pj} in such a way due to the fact that it is hard to choose better (good) nodes to perform routing. Focusing only on the nodes network interface queue is complex to judge and to select better nodes for routing. For example, routing is performed through a node with 95% queue utilization and at this criterion, check whether the network interface queue utilization is lower than the threshold value or not. If it is lower than the threshold value, then it is not so much important to distinguish nodes based on their network interface queue utilization. The threshold parameter 11 is set to a measure the real-interval [0.1, 1.0] and therefore, it can control the *suppressing effect* while routing through the paths comprised with maximum network interface queue utilization nodes. If 11 is set to smaller value, then the considered-node should possess lower network interface queue utilization in order to achieve $LS_m^{Pj} = 1.0$. If 11 is set to greater value, then the considered-node should possess maximum 'network interface queue utilization' in order to achieve $LS_m^{Pj} = 1.0$. Conversely, when routing is done through jammed (congested) nodes, the suppressing effect is higher with lower 11 value. As per the choice, the value of 11 can be set even to '1.0'. During this process, the degeneration of the CALARM routing-metric occurs without considering the workload of the nodes(Yuan et al,2017) . Therefore, it should be careful that the suppressing effect should not be too greater, moderate, or too low same as 0.6 for 11 (i.e. the value of 11 used in our simulation studies is selected based on wish).

Furthermore, Equation (5.3) states the metric value of the considerable path which is given by $CALARM_{p_j}$ and it simplifies the sum of $(1-P_{ENC_m}^{p_j})/LS_m^{p_j}$ at the intermediate nodes and the source available in the path.

$(1-P^{p_j}$

$$CALARM_{p_j} = \sum_{m \in p_j, m \le dist(p_j)} \frac{ENC_m}{LS_m^{p_j}} \tag{5.3}$$

The path with minimum CALARM value requires minimum number of transmissions to send a packet from the source to their respective destination. Net-CART protocol wishes to transmit its packet through path with minimum CALARM value. By this, the source nodes do not accept the shorter paths and the path with many coding opportunities. They avoid the paths with congested nodes for packet transmission. In other words, it can be said that the source nodes select the optimal path for packet transmission.

S.4.4 Rvroup Mechanism

Owing to the route discovery process, the RREQ source tries to identify more number of available paths to the RREQ destination. Moreover, the RREP while traversing from the RREQ destination to the RREQ sources, it is possible to compute the CALARM value of a path. On the other hand, employing a new control packet named as RvRoup (Reverse-Route-Update), the CALARM value of a path can be easily computed and updated periodically. In Net-CART, the incoming paths are monitored by the nodes and to the source nodes, the RvRoup is transmitted periodically with an end goal to update the 'routing metric' values of the paths at the 'source nodes'. The RvRoup structure is more similar to the RREP structure. The nodes can also be updated with the current information concerning the neighbors of their downstream nodes using this newly proposed RvRoup mechanism. Using this RvRoup method, a source node receives the latest information about the network and also based on the CLARAM routing-metric, the source node selects the most ideal path for the transmission of packets.

S.S SIMULATION ENVIRONMENT AND PERFORMANCE EVALUATION

The Net-CART protocol is evaluated using NS2 simulator. The performance of the proposed Net-CART protocol is evaluated under two different types of networks such as a) grid-network and b) random-network.

A network called random-network is used to evaluate the performance of the proposed Net-CART protocol. More importantly, in each network about 100 nodes are distributed randomly in 1000x1000m^2 area. This aims to generate a partitioned network because, the partitioned networks could make the result analysis as a tedious process. For each flow, about 10 pairs of nodes are selected randomly as its sources and destinations. For each flow rate, the simulation results are analyzed over 20-scenarios.

In Net - Cart, all the nodes are connected with promiscuous mode in order to save all the packets for further analysis with a customized IEEE 802.11 standard, as the MAC protocol carries the opportunistic transmission. User Datagram Protocol (UDP) has been utilized as traffic sources, and all the flows

A. Throughput

Throughput is one of the important parameters for evaluating the performance. Throughput is calculated based on number of bits transmitted per second. In order to provide better performance of the network, the system throughput must be high. The performance of Net-CART has been analyzed in a larger random mesh network in which 100 nodes with the size of 1,000 x 1,000 have been constructed and also, 5 by 5 grid topology has been constructed where each node can reach its surrounding neighboring nodes. The experiments are conducted over 100 nodes for 20 rounds. At every round, 5 flows are added randomly into the network and the same process is repeated for 3 times. The Figures 5.6 and 5.7 show the performance comparison of the existing FORM algorithm and the proposed Net-CART routing algorithm based on transmission rate for random topology and grid topology for100 nodes. It can be noted from the Figure 5.6 and Figure 5.7, that the throughput through the proposed Net-CART is gradually increasing compared to the existing FORM routing algorithm. By the proposed Net-CART, the best coding opportunity paths are identified using Code-Aware and Load-Aware (CALARM) route metrics. Numerous coding structures are identified and more numbers of packets encodings have been supported using Enhanced Universal Coding Strategies (EUCS). Therefore, the proposed Net-CART gives better throughput using network coding in wireless mesh networks.

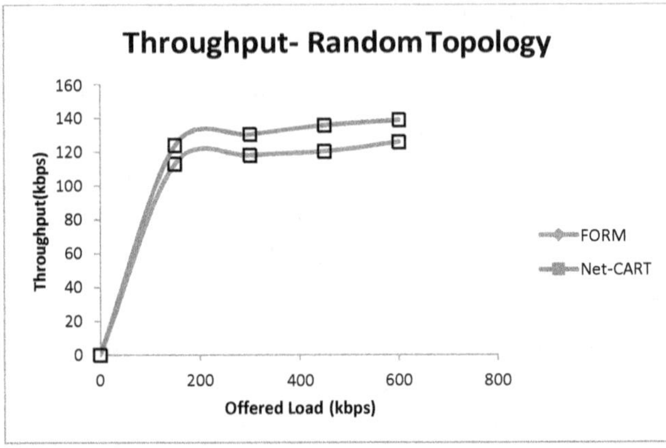

Figure S.6 Throughput of FORM and Net-CART for random topology

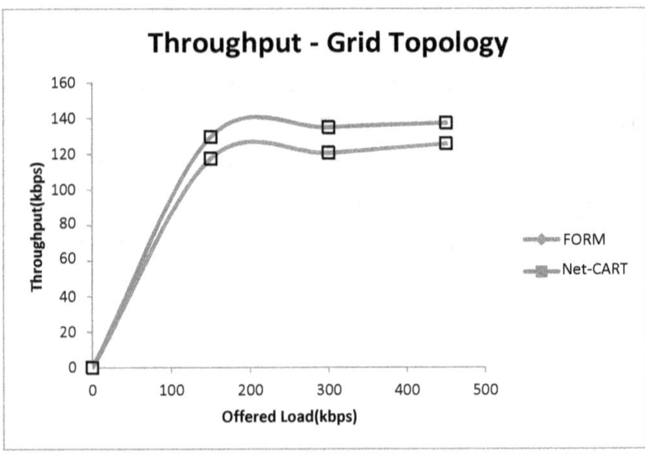

Figure S.7 Throughput of FORM and Net-CART for grid topology

B. End-to-End delay

The ratio of packet received time to the packet sent time is termed as end-to-end delay. The Figure 5.8 and Figure 5.9 show the performance graphs of routing end-to-end delay in continuous traffic pattern for the existing FORM algorithm and the proposed Net-CART routing algorithm for random and grid for 100 nodes .

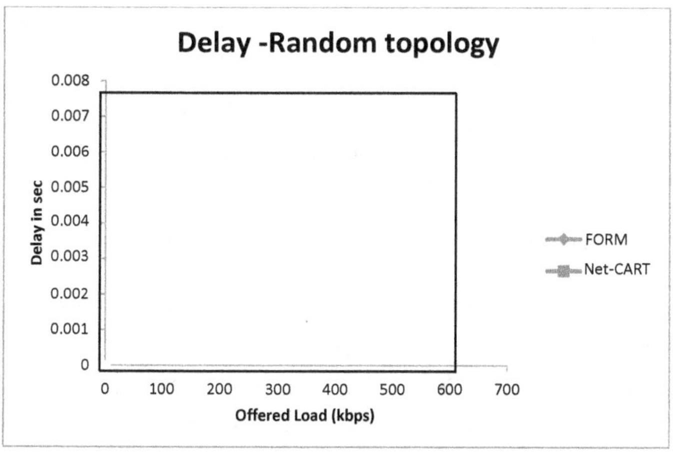

Figure S.8 Delay of FORM and Net-CART for random topology

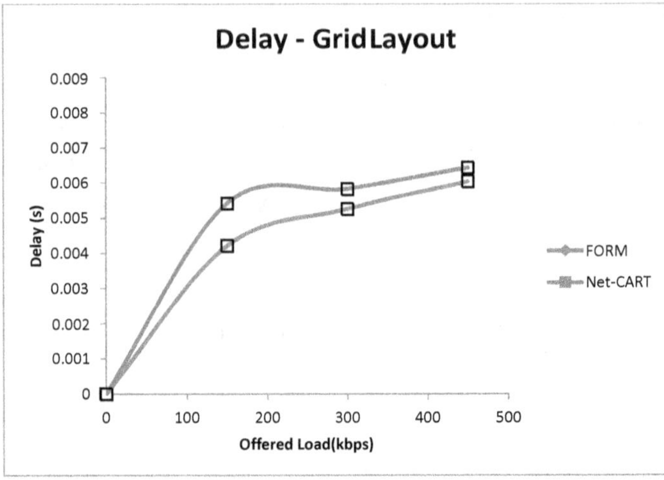

Figure 5.9 Delay of FORM and Net-CART for grid topology

Due to the EUCS coding structures, Net-CART algorithm has exhibited better performance compared to the FORM but Net-CART algorithm experiences slightly higher packet delay than FORM, because Net-CART protocol largely involves to gain more packet delivery ratio by sending more number of packets successfully to their respective destination.

C. Packet Delivery Ratio

The packet delivery ratio is defined as the ratio of number of packets successfully received by the destination to those generated by the source. The performance graphs in Figure 5.10 and Figure 5.11 represent the packet delivery ratio of the existing FORM algorithm and the proposed Net-CART algorithm with respect to speed for random and grid topologies for 100 nodes. It is inferred that the proposed Net-CART protocol not only identifies more coding-structures (i.e. the unique ways the packets encoded collectively) but also follows the coding-structures to generate more packet-encodings. From the

Figures, it can be observed that the newly developed CALARM routing-metric of Net-CART achieves the goal of a source node by selecting the shorter paths with many coding-opportunities for packet transmission and avoids the selection of paths with more congested nodes in the network to achieve higher packet delivery ratio.

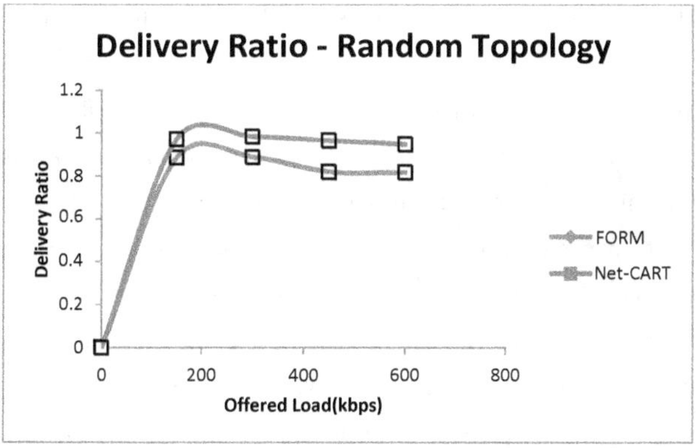

Figure S.10 Packet Delivery Ratio of FORM and Net-CART for random topology

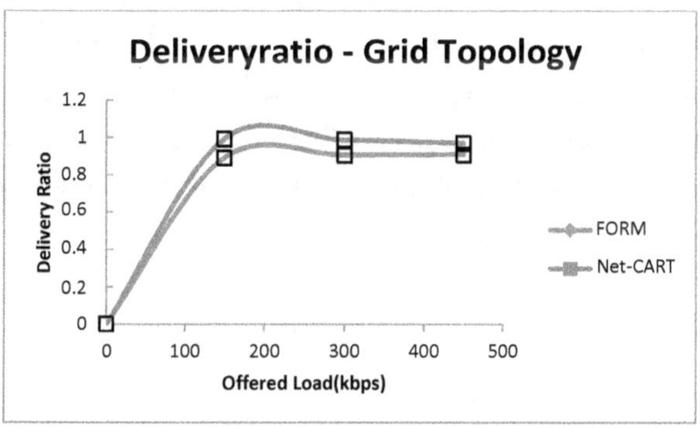

Figure S.11 Packet Delivery Ratio of FORM and Net-CART for grid topology

S.6 SUMMARY

The problems of coding strategies employed for throughput improvement are studied and a new Net-CART (Network Coding Aware Routing) protocol has been proposed by considering the goodness of network-coding. Moreover, WMNs suffer from low network throughput because of its multi-hop communication characteristics, whereas this type of communication demands more number of packet transmissions for the successful deliverance of packets to the destination. Network-coding can be used to increase the network throughput in WMNs, due to the fact that it minimizes the packet transmission count required to deliver certain number of packets to destination. While employing network coding in WMNs, there are several challenges and that should be met such as i) identifying packets that can be combined (encoded) collectively and ii) integrating the coding strategies in routing protocols. A new mesh routing algorithm, that integrates network-coding called as Net-CART, has been proposed to improve the performance of Wireless Mesh Networks. To utilize the whole benefit of network coding, the Net-CART algorithm uses a novel routing metric called CALARM. Additionally, to find numerous coding structures and to support number of packet encodings, an improved set of coding strategies known as EUCS has been proposed. An extensive simulation study has been carried out on wide range of network configurations and from the study, it is observed that the proposed Net-CART algorithm has attained higher throughput compared to FORM routing algorithm.

CHAPTER 6

EMPIRICAL SURVEY AND COMPARISION OF PROPOSED FRAMEWORKS

INTRODUCTION

Wireless mesh networks are dynamically self-organized and self-configured and also nodes in the WMNs establish and maintain the mesh connectivity among them automatically. Because of that WMNs have low up-front cost, robustness, reliable service coverage and easy maintenance (Akyilidze *et al.* 2005). Routers in a mesh networks act as hosts and also forward packets. In this chapter, assessments of the proposed routing algorithm frameworks are presented: OEDAR, ACAR, Net-CART routing algorithm which have been incorporated in the previous chapters. Purposely, experiments have been carried out with the intention of achieving an empirical appraisal of the proposed three frameworks, assessing the efficiency of the proposed three sets of features and its comparison with throughput, delay and packet delivery ratio for these proposed algorithms.

PARAMETERS USED IN THE PROPOSED WORKS

In this frame work, the performance of three prominent routing algorithm OEDAR, ACAR, Net-CART were compared. The work has been carried out by using NS-2 simulator, random waypoint mobility model. The outcome of simulation parameters illustrates the importance of evaluating and implementing routing algorithms in wireless mesh network environment. The objective of the thesis is to select best encoding node with more coding opportunistic and improves the gain of the opportunistic transmission using OEDAR, ACAR and Net-CART routing algorithm. In order to fulfil the objective a comparative analysis between these three routing algorithm has to be carried out in the simulated environment created in the NS2 discrete event network simulator, comprising of 100 mobile nodes based on the three basic parameters throughput, packet delivery ratio and delay. Comparisons made with respect simulation parameters. NS2 simulator are widely used to evaluate network routing algorithms and protocols. They have considerable advantages compared to other methodologies such as real-time experiments and mathematical modelling. A theoretical study has been made and tested the intended methods empirically in a network simulator. The performance of OEDAR,ACAR and Net-CART routing algorithms with respect to packet delivery ratio, end to end delay and throughput is compared.

6.2.1 Performance Metrics

For evaluation of the proposed quality constraints routing algorithms, three metrics: throughput, packet delivery ratio and delay are considered. The simulation parameters are summarized in Table 6.1.

Table 6.1 simulation Parameters

Parameters	values
Simulation area	1000m X 1000m
Simulator	NS-2
MAC type	802.11
Propagation Model	Two ray
Traffic type	CBR
Antenna model	Omni directional
Node Placement	Random
Number of nodes	100
Transmission range	250m
Mobility Model	Random way point model
Simulation duration	500s

Throughput

It is defined as total number of packets received by the destination node. It is a measure of efficiency of a routing protocol. There is two representations of throughput one is the amount of data transferred over the period of time expressed in kilobits per second (Kbps). The other is the packet delivery percentage obtained from a ratio of the number of data packets sent and the number of data packets received.

Throughput performance comparison Metrics for HCOR, OEDAR, F-ACAR, S-ACAR, FORM, Net-CART algorithms are shown in Figure 6.2.

Table 6.2 Throughput comparison for various routing algorithms

S.no	Load (kbs)	HCOR		OEDAR		F-ACAR		S-ACAR		FORM		Net-CART	
		RT	GT	RT	GT	RT	GT	RT	GT	RT	GT	RT	GT
1	150	89.94	108.56	99.95	115.7	101.65	91.89	101.88	115.98	112.9	117.6	123.9	129.7
2	300	89.99	101.72	111.42	113.1	111.89	92.03	112.48	114.99	117.9	120.7	130.4	135.1
3	450	88.27	100.91	111.72	110.4	112.35	93.05	112.98	114.74	120.3	125.9	135.7	137.5
4	600	87.72	100.64	112.73	110.8	114.42	93.99	114.97	113.89	125.8	127.6	138.7	145.8

Table 6.2 gives the result of throughput and it is observed that, Net-CART algorithms exhibited better performance when compared to the other algorithms. After comparison, it inferred that, at maximum workload the total network throughput and the packet delivery ratio obtained in the grid test are higher than those that obtained in random test. This limitation in random topology occurs, because of higher nodal den sity than that in the grid-network. In addition to this, more interference and higher channel contention is experienced with random distribution of nodes in a plane (i.e. nodes are concentrated more in some areas). Hence, with grid-network the nodes are distributed periodically and there may be less possibility for interference and higher channel contention as much as in the random-network.

Packet Delivery Ratio

The ratio between the number of packets originated by the CBR sources and the number of packets received by the CBR sink at the final destination. It describes the loss rate seen by the algorithms.

Packet delivery ratio metrics for HCOR, OEDAR, F-ACAR, S-ACAR, FORM, Net-CART algorithms are compared in table 6.3.

Table 6.3 packet delivery ratio results for various routing algorithms

S.no	Load (kbs)	HCOR		OEDAR		F-ACAR		S-ACAR		FORM		Net-CART	
		RT	GT	RT	GT	RT	GT	RT	GT	RT	GT	RT	GT
1	150	81.66	89.43	90.90	97.8	91.89	98.45	92.98	98.99	88.66	89.04	97.21	99.20
2	300	82.89	90.59	92.85	98.6	92.03	98.95	93.58	98.9	88.94	90.59	98.45	98.6
3	450	82.05	91.82	92.57	98.4	93.05	98.31	93.96	98.62	82.05	90.8	97.57	96.93
4	600	81.78	92.13	92.88	98.46	93.99	98.26	94.09	98.46	81.77	91.13	95.88	96.47

Table 6.3 gives the result of packet delivery ratio for various routing algorithms with respect to offered load. It is observed that, Net-CART routing algorithm has delivered more packets at the destination compared to other algorithms. Compared to HCOR algorithms, OEDAR and ACAR have more packet delivery ratio significantly. It observed that, Net-CART algorithm not only identifies more coding-structures (i.e. the unique ways the packets encoded collectively) but also follows the coding-structures to generate more packet-encodings.

End-to-End Delay

It is the average time taken for a packet to travel from source node to a destination node. It includes all probable delays caused by buffering during route discovery latency, queuing at the interface queue, rebroadcast on delays at MAC, propagation and transfer times. End-to-end delay performances for HCOR, OEDAR, F-ACAR, S-ACAR, FORM, Net-CART algorithms are compared in table 6.4.

Table 6.4 Performance comparisons of end-to-end delay for various algorithms.

S.no	Load (kbs)	HCOR (delay in ms)		OEDAR (delay in ms)		F-ACAR (delay in ms)		S-ACAR (delay in ms)		FORM (delay in ms)		Net-CART (delay in ms)	
		RT	GT	RT	GT	RT	GT	RT	GT	RT	GT	RT	GT
1	150	5.06	5.89	3.82	4.62	4.01	4.73	4.31	4.80	4.021	4.22	4.685	5.42
2	300	5.70	6.01	4.16	4.90	4.26	4.82	4.50	4.90	5.25	5.26	5.75	5.83
3	450	6.29	6.14	4.43	5.09	4.53	4.90	4.83	5.09	6.44	6.04	6.85	6.43
4	600	6.43	6.22	4.78	5.18	4.84	4.99	5.01	5.25	7.04	7.02	7.50	7.34

Table 6.4 gives the result of end-to-end delay for various algorithms. It is observed that OEDAR routing algorithm has minimum delay compared to other algorithms. Net-CART algorithm experience, slightly higher packet delay than other routing algorithms because Net-CART algorithm largely involves to gain more packet delivery ratio by sending more number of packets successfully to their respective destination and it has larger routing overhead compared to other algorithms.

SUMMARY

Simulations are run to examine the algorithms performance. From Table 6.2, 6.3 and 6.4, it can be concluded that the proposed algorithms are compared with HCOR algorithms. OEDAR algorithm has been used for delay-aware routing packet transmissions and also shortest range of packet transmission. F-ACAR and S-ACAR algorithms are used for code-aware and delay-aware routing packet transmissions because they have moderate throughput gain and delay values compared to other routing algorithms. Net-CART algorithm is proposed for code-aware and load-aware packet transmissions because it uses load-aware route metric which prevents the source node to transmit their packet in the path with large number of congested nodes and also follows the coding- structures to generate more packet-encodings. An improvement in packet delivery ratio and throughput are observed in the proposed Net-CART routing algorithm.

CHAPTER 7

CONCLUSION AND FUTURE WORK

CONCLUSION

This chapter summarizes the complete works established in the thesis. In this research work, various network coding techniques that include an Opportunity Encoder based Delay Aware Routing algorithm (OEDAR) for enhancing the throughput and reducing the delay using network coding in wireless mesh networks, Adaptive coding Aware Routing Algorithm (ACAR) to encode the packets in two different flows that will not have the intermediate nodes, Network coding aware routing algorithm (Net-CART) to avail the whole goodness of network-coding technique to increase the quantity of coding-opportunities in wireless mesh networks have been proposed. These techniques are used to achieve better performance in terms of throughput and packet delivery ratio as well as reducing delay consumption with increasing nodes compared to the existing protocol. The existing works on the network coding, route metrics, opportunistic routing algorithms are analyzed.

A new distributed routing algorithm OEDAR has been designed using anypath routing cost in which each node performs the coding opportunity and chooses the appropriate route by itself using the information obtained from its neighbors and the feedback from intersecting nodes in its routes. OEDAR intends to resolve whether the network coding is supposed to be done based on the coding conditions and which nodes ought to be used as the encoding nodes to obtain the highest throughput gain. To realize OEDAR, every encoded node within two hop region will get selected and also each node performs the computation of temporary anypath cost and total delay independently for each encoded flow using Optimal Encoder Selection (OES) algorithm. Anypath routing cost is computed from Expected Transmission count (ETX) and weighted average cost of the node. All flows constantly choose the lowest anypath cost path and minimal delay as their transmission route. Prior to network coding, the coding node must ensure whether the encoded flow is decodable which means at least one node in the backward list is able to decode this encoded flow. To ensure this, the coding node must have the decoding knowledge before taking any coding decision. OEDAR is able to handle diverse environments, such as multiple flow rates and multiple coding nodes along the route. Simulation of the proposed routing protocol has been carried out under NS-2 simulator. The results show that OEDAR outperforms HCOR by selecting one node that has minimum delay and the lowest any path cost has been chosen among all the intersecting nodes. Moreover, higher throughput, low end-to-end delay and high packet delivery ratio are achieved through the proposed OEDAR algorithm.

Then a new improved Adaptive coding aware routing algorithm (ACAR) has been designed by considering anypath routing cost, delay and bandwidth of selected flow. This study also establishes and observes an optimal encoder node for two distinct flows that will not have the intermediate node in wireless mesh networks. The proposed encoder node selection algorithm has been projected to improve the performance of routing protocol for the transmission of packets in wireless mesh networks. Among all possible paths, the anypath is selected based on the shortest Expected Transmission Count (ETX). In any path routing, an intermediate node receives a packet from a flow only when the destination and neighbors are in the downstream of this flow. According to the Adaptive optimal encoder coding condition in ACAR algorithm, the potential decoding nodes of this packet should be either in destination or in one hop before destination. ACAR algorithm is applied, when two flows don't have the intermediate node but have the common overhearing node for any one of the flow. S-ACAR algorithm is applicable only when two flows have common overhearing node in the network. Then, any one of the optimal nodes, which should be placed in neighbor list of two flows has to be selected and it should also satisfy the coding condition. The performance results of ACAR give better results by improving the average throughput and packet delivery ratio and reducing delay consumption with increasing nodes compared to the existing protocol. ACAR uses the optimal encoder coding condition to maximize the throughput and minimize the delay.

Experimentation has been done, and this work shows higher performance of packet delivery ratio compared to other network coding routing algorithms. It also it gives better results by providing less end-to-end delay, higher throughput and higher packet delivery ratio compared to other multipath routings protocols.

Further a proposed Network coding aware routing (Net-CART) protocol in wireless mesh networks has been proposed and that considers the scenario has more than two flows intersect at one node. An improved set of coding strategies called Enhanced Universal Coding strategies (EUCS) have also been proposed to determine large number of coding opportunities. A node in the Net-CART approach adapts the EUCS to find whether the packets can be 'encoded' collectively or not. Beyond this newly developed coding strategies, a new metric Code-Aware and Load-Aware Route Metric (CALARM) has been developed to utilize the whole goodness of network coding and to enhance the network throughput. CALARM is modeled based on small amount of transmission and the coding opportunities are considered to transmit a packet from source to its respective destination. The path with minimum CALARM value requires minimum number of transmissions to send a packet from the source to their respective destination. Hence, the source node selects the optimal path for packet transmission. A new control packet RvRoup (Reverse-Route-Update) is employed to easily compute the CALARM value of a path and it is updated periodically. Using this RvRoup method, a source node receives the latest information about the network and also based on the CALARM routing metric, the source node selects the most ideal path for the transmission of packets. Following the basics of Dynamic Source Routing (DSR) and FORM protocol, the Net-CART has been proposed for perfect transmission of packets to the destination. The proposed Net-CART protocol has attained higher throughput compared to other routing protocols like DSR, FORM, MRA and MRT. Net-CART protocol not only identifies more coding-structures (i.e. the unique ways the packets encoded collectively) but also follows the coding-structures to generate more packet-encodings. From the experimentation, it is clear that this work offers higher performance of packet delivery ratio compared to other network coding routing algorithms. It also gives better results by providing less end-to-end delay, higher throughput and higher packet delivery ratio compared to other multipath routings protocols.

FUTURE WORK

To an efficient coding-aware opportunistic scheme may be designed with encoding of more than two native flows together and also this Net-CART protocol may be executed on a 'real' and 'prototype' based test beds. The experiments will be improved to verify its flexibility and practicality. Moreover, physical network-coding may be introduced in future research.

The analysis of network coding algorithms could be valuable for future coding-aware opportunistic routing design when it extends the design of coding-aware opportunistic schemes with encoding of multiple native flows together. Implement and evaluate network coding on top of a variety of MAC protocols including 802.11 are planned for future work. Within the cross-layer optimization philosophy, designing a MAC protocol that contributes in creating information diversity in the network is considered to work and thus, making network coding more powerful. To obtain the expressions for most favorable number of sources as well as their best possible placement for a given deployment of nodes in future. Investigate the delay- throughput tradeoffs in the case of hop-by-hop retransmissions. Correlation of losses among the paths issues and study of paths that contain links with bursty errors are considered as a future research.

www.ingramcontent.com/pod-product-compliance
Lightning Source LLC
LaVergne TN
LVHW052306200926
848481LV00002B/483